Haga's Law

Haga's Law

Why Nothing Works and No One Can Fix It and the More We Try the Worse It Gets

by
Dr. William James Haga
and Nicholas Acocella

Illustrated by Randall Hylkema

William Morrow and Company, Inc.
New York 1980

Library of Congress Cataloging in Publication Data

Haga, William James.
　　Haga's law.

　　Includes bibliographical references and index.
　　1. Bureaucracy—Anecdotes, facetiae, satire, etc.　2. Organization—
Anecdotes, facetiae, satire, etc.　3. Anxiety—Anecdotes, facetiae, satire,
etc.　I. Acocella, Nicholas, joint author.　II. Title.
✓ HM131.H226　　　　301.18′32　　　　79-19353
ISBN 0-688-03542-6

Book Design by Michael Mauceri

Printed in the United States of America.

First Edition

1　2　3　4　5　6　7　8　9　10

To Carline and Joan

Contents

*With few exceptions, examples used in **Haga's Law** are actual events or composites of a category of actual events. In some cases we have conceded to counsel that we disguise real people and organizations, using obviously fictional names, in order to protect the guilty.*

—DR. WILLIAM JAMES HAGA AND
NICHOLAS ACOCELLA

Haga's Law

Chapter 1

Haga's Law

Why Bureaucracy Is Inevitable

Four be the things I'd been better without:
Love, curiosity, freckles, and doubt.
— Dorothy Parker

Nothing works and no one can fix it. We have all observed the phenomenon, perhaps the central reality of our time.

A thirsty man craves water.

In an earlier time he would have dug a well.

Today he must be content that the response to his thirst is the establishment of a Regional Water Resources Management Control Board.

The wonder is that he is not only content but deeply gratified, so seductive is the organizing addiction.

Mankind seeks solutions but gets organizations instead.

Modern man bows to silly rules, drowns in meticulous regulations, suffers tedious meetings, and submits to procedures that impose more social costs than they prevent.

We can observe two facts.

(*1*) Everyone detests bureaucracy.

(*2*) Bureaucracy is spreading like a prairie fire into every corner of work and play.

We can no longer avoid the paradox: if bureaucracy is so evil, why is it so prevalent?

Four Representative Cases

In our scientific study of mankind's addiction to organizing, we collected data on hundreds of case studies. Four of

them will suffice to portray what a carload of correlation coefficients could not illuminate.

REGIMENT PARK PUBLIC SCHOOL SYSTEM. Faced with dropping enrollment and a consequent cutback in budget, the officials in the Regiment Park school system reacted in the only way they could. They hired specialists to write proposals to get federal money. They formed co-ordinating committees to optimize available resources. They appointed fact-finding task forces. They planned new departments to find ways of reducing the student dropout rate.

Consequently, secretaries in the school system were burdened by a blizzard of paperwork: status reports, numerical evaluations, budget analyses, memoranda, project schedules, committee agenda, and speeches to community groups on "The Crisis in Public Education." The threat of fiscal peril in Regiment Park's schools was smothered with a flourishing bureaucracy.

WHISTLEHALT OBEDIENCE CLUB. Five years ago, Dogwood bought a German Shepherd puppy. In seeking to have his pup trained, he discovered that the price of a private obedience tutorial was forbidding. Dogwood joined with four other puppy owners in similar straits to hire a dog trainer. Each of them ended up with a trained dog and an intact budget.

Things did not stop there, however. Fearing that thousands of puppies throughout Whistlehalt would be deprived of the same inexpensive training which their own dogs enjoyed, Dogwood and friends formed the Whistlehalt Obedience Club. The club hired trainers and offered regularly scheduled group-rate obedience classes. Hundreds of potentially unruly beasts became useful companions.

THE COZY CO-OP. In an effort to hold down the prohibitive costs of housing in New York City, eight families formed a co-op corporation, bought an old building, and converted it into eight apartments. Their plan was to manage and maintain the building themselves, with everyone sharing in the work on an equal basis.

State law required their corporation to have a board of directors and officers. Four residents served on the first board, which established a Janitor-of-the-Month duty roster. In addition, the president appointed standing committees on heating, maintenance, charter revision, legal affairs, lobby renovation, and social activities. You can't rely on friendship alone to get the garbage out. For that you need a hierarchy, however small.

MUTCHADOO STATE UNIVERSITY. Four years ago, students at Mutchadoo State informally evaluated classroom teaching. At the end of each term, anonymous remarks were collected about each professor's methods, personal traits, textbooks, and tests. These were sold to fellow students as a consumer guide.

Many instructors were shaken by the broadcasting of candid reports of their clumsy ways in the classroom. The faculty quickly perceived the whole evaluation business as a threat. Acting decisively, they formed a committee, the Faculty Committee on Instructional Evaluation. The committee quickly metamorphosed into a permanent Office of Instructional Evaluation. The Office first banned student involvement in rating teachers, then took over the student rating system, lock, stock, and computer-readable forms. When last seen the Office of Instructional Evaluation was getting by with a dean of instructional evaluation, three associate deans, a pool of secretaries, and a legion of computer programmers.

Our meticulously scientific study of these cases—and hundreds of others—has revealed a common thread of human motivation: people organize out of a dread of uncertainty. Mankind simply cannot leave well enough alone.

The Best Surprise Is No Surprise

With scarce exception, children in the United States play baseball within the structure of the Little League. Gone are the spontaneous games in vacant lots or level pastures without safety equipment, adult umpires, trophies, stadium lights, and racial balance. Only by organizing are such benefactions secured. Not to organize is to leave things to chance.

Americans shun adventures such as dining at Maud's Gas & Eat in Prairie Heights. No matter that Maud's could be a culinary delight; travelers universally prefer the standardized menu at the Golden Arches fast-food establishments. Monotony is invariably preferred to uncertainty.

Election campaigns in the United States are run by organizations approaching the size of an army. "Advance men" move ahead of their candidates, sweeping away land mines of uncertainty lurking in the well-meaning incompetence of local party volunteers. Welcoming crowds are drummed up to assure that spontaneous hurrahs are well rehearsed. Few are more possessed of an itch to organize than political candidates; few have so much riding on the wind of uncertainty.

However widely endorsed the proverb "Variety is the spice of life," the multitude acts out a preference for blander fare. In the elegant phrasing of a hotel chain's advertising slogan, "The best surprise is no surprise."

Jody's Syndrome

Every disease has its fund-raising organization. Most mammals have a hierarchical shield of organized benefactors.

Many fish have one too. Bureaucracy has now come to the aid of amphibians, as well.

In 1976, Jimmy Carter's press aide, Jody Powell, fell to verbal combat with rival Georgian Lester Maddox when the latter tried to derail the Carter campaign in New Hampshire. Powell asserted that "being called a liar by Lester Maddox was like being called ugly by a frog."

That was when we all learned of the power of organized frog lovers, who drove Powell to apologize publicly—not to Maddox but to the frogs of America.

Songster Randy Newman stepped into a similar cow pie when he released a recording forthrightly entitled "Short People." When this lyrical bit of size-forty-two-extra-long chauvinism hit the airwaves, Newman quickly became aware of the Little People of America, organized representative of citizens under four feet eleven inches in height. Pressure from the tall-talking Little People drove the song off the air.

A Relentless Trend

Life is more organized this year than it was last year. It will be still more so next year.

Even the institution of the family—the last bastion of non-bureaucratic functioning—has succumbed to formalization, its traditional duties having been systematically commandeered by formal organizations.

Planned Parenthood suggests the correct number of children.

Lamaze training shows how to bear them.

The La Leche League tells how to breast-feed them.

Parent Effectiveness Training reveals methods of guiding children who won't clean their rooms.

Day-care centers and preschools replace the fabled grandmothers and kindly aunts of yore.

A Federal hot-lunch program takes the element of risk out of the traditional motherly brown bag.*

A Web Is Being Spun Across the Land

Far and wide, the same processes are at work.
Small is becoming big.
Simple is growing complicated.
Easy is surrendering to difficult.
Fun is being displaced by drudgery.
Purpose is giving way to procedure.
A web of over-organization is being spun across the land.

Committees, officials, rules, and organizations proliferate, pushing into the last informal corners of everyday life. Spontaneity is being driven from its last sanctuaries. Recently, street musicians in San Francisco—symbols of unorganized entertainment—fell under the licensing powers of the municipal government.

Not to be outdone, the Oklahoma House of Representatives debated a proposal to require a male to obtain a female's signature on an official consent form—in duplicate—before an act of sexual intercourse.

No island of spontaneity will be safe from the spread of the organizing addiction.

Yet everyone we questioned was quick to say that he, personally, is one of the best friends spontaneity ever had. In every case, the blame was laid on the wickedness of others.

On the one hand, spontaneity has no enemies. On the other, it is being snuffed out right and left. No one loves

* The one family-related activity even callous system watchers never imagined succumbing to organization was adultery. They were wrong. Whereas extramarital promiscuity was once spontaneous, today couples searching for a night of controlled and simultaneous philandering in New York or Los Angeles join a swinging club.

bureaucracy, but it abounds. No one hates spontaneity, but it shrivels. Indeed, it will soon disappear altogether.

Only after intensive study did we discover the key to this paradox: *spontaneity is being loved to death.*

Two Propensities

Spontaneity is not being choked by a dark conspiracy. On the contrary, we are all accessories to its vanishment. Wittingly or not, people everywhere are freezing carefree pursuits into committees, agenda, hierarchies, rule books, and specialties. The saplings of bureaucracy are cultivated with good intentions.

Bureaucracy is a social machine invented to assure certainty by driving out the threat of things unforeseen. Officialdom is a monument to mankind's flight from puzzlement and anxiety to the Promised Land of predictability.

Organizing is the natural—and virtually the only—response to a world of threats and fears.

Years of studying organizations—large and small, private and public—have led unswervingly to one conclusion: as the Regiment Park schools, the Whistlehalt Obedience Club, the Cozy Co-op, and Mutchadoo State University go, so goes the world. As nature abhors a vacuum, humankind abhors the anxiety of leaving things to chance. It is the iron law of human behavior. It is the germ of the organizing addiction, the driving force behind the rush to bureaucracy.

The evidence has compelled us to offer the ground-breaking scientific expression of this universal urge as the *First Propensity*:

Anxiety Begets Organizing.

Regulations, procedures, offices, jurisdictions, controls, checks, audits, forms, coordinating committees, approvals, schedules, reports, and the other paraphernalia of organizing exist only to exorcise the hobgoblin of anxiety. Not to embrace these incremental degrees of formalization, not to taste the sweet liqueur of organizing, is to entertain anxiety by leaving things to chance. Nothing will be left to chance. Everything will be left to organizing.

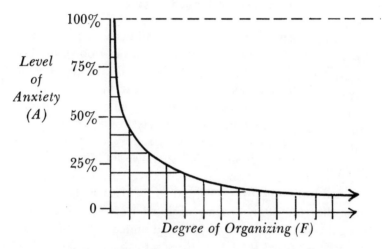

Figure 1. The Effect of Organizing upon Anxiety

The effect of organizing upon anxiety can be readily grasped in Figure 1, in which the more perceptive reader will observe that the first degrees of organizing reduce anxiety to an astonishingly satisfactory level. So long as *any* level of anxiety remains, however, still further degrees of structure and formalizing must be applied. Yet, each such application yields progressively less and less in the way of reducing anxiety. Nevertheless, the compulsion to organize, reorganize, and over-organize is not diminished. On the contrary! The itch to regiment and systemize is only aggravated, pushing bureaucratization to yet greater lengths in pursuit of the last breath of uncertainty.

The Other Shoe

The weight of the data that compelled the formulation of the First Propensity also pressed us to make a general expression of its corollary, the *Second Propensity*:

Organizing Begets Anxiety.

We found again and again that the addictive push to over-organize every threat into submission and hunt down the last traces of unpredictability only confronted anxiety-aversive organizers with new anxieties. Indeed, the burden of many of the pages that follow is to reveal systematically the details —step-by-step—of this pernicious process.

In what soon enough becomes an orgy of diminishing returns, organizers hound the shadows of happenstance throughout their fattening administrative labyrinths. Having succeeded in extinguishing 90 percent of the risk in running things, they too often become obsessed with the idea of defeating the last 10 percent. So obsessed, indeed, that they drift into careless regard for larger threats to their domains. Pursuit of small threats renders administrators ripe for being astounded by big ones. It is ever so.*

The Paradox Resolved

Mankind disparages bureaucracy. Everyone can recite an inventory of its vices. Yet, as all can plainly see, spontaneous endeavors are swept away by a rising flood of authority hierarchies and rationalized processes. Together, the First and

---

* The harsh consequences of the Second Propensity are mirrored in the Quicksand Corollary (Chapter 5) and disclosed in finer theoretical detail and fascinating application as the Dumb conclusion to the Fat, Happy, and Dumb Process (Chapter 16). Its inescapable truth is contained in the explication of Acocella's Axiom in the same chapter.

Second Propensities resolve the paradox: humanity's disdain for bureaucratic systems is surpassed only by its horror of events it cannot predict or things it cannot control. Yet, uncertainty remains a constant. The triumph of systems and hierarchies over chance and hazard, in turn, propels human ventures straight into new crises fraught with chance and hazards.

The Law Revealed

While the two Propensities have been divulged separately for the sake of patient explanation, in reality they are two sides of a single principle, *Haga's Law*:

Anxiety Begets Organizing;

Organizing Begets Anxiety.

Chapter 2
The Organizing Trap

How Nice Little Groups Are Turned into Big Bad Bureaucracies

All this struggling and striving to make the world better is a great mistake; . . . because striving and struggling is the worst way you can set about doing anything.
—George Bernard Shaw

When things are going right, no one can resist the urge to keep them going. Compassion and self-interest dictate that a good thing must be helped to survive and prosper. Survival demands more than spontaneity. The survival of good things can leave nothing to chance. The sentiments that are good enough to, say, bring parents and teachers together once cannot be trusted to bring them together regularly. For that you must organize a Parent-Teachers Association.

To Love Something Is to Organize It

Good things usually start as spontaneous events or informal gatherings. Unencumbered by formal procedures, communication blocks, or the brier patch of internal politics, an informal group can strike swiftly to solve problems, crystallize fleeting opinions, and promote spur-of-the-moment fun. Things go so well in these warm little groups, however, that everyone wants to preserve what they have created. The only way to save a good thing is to organize it.

26

That is the *Organizing Trap*:

If Something Is Good, Keep It Going; To Keep It Going, Organize It.

Certainly, cheap and accessible training for rowdy dogs in Whistlehalt would not exist today if Dogwood had been content to leave things to chance alone.

Imagine the effect upon the club's future had Dogwood handled publicity, to mention but one vital function, merely by sighing offhandedly to Barkdale, "You know, I think a lot more people would show up for the obedience classes if we could just get a story in the Sunday magazine of the Whistlehalt *Herald*; what do you think?"

Could Dogwood have gone about his other presidential duties assured that his barely uttered wish would become, for Barkdale, an explicit command? Of course not! Down that path lies uncertainty. The Organizing Trap drives Dogwood to fix the publicity chore upon Barkdale and to hold him accountable for the results.

Busting Out All Over

No sooner has the noble urge to preserve a good thing been fulfilled than it is succeeded by still another motive, equally laudable, the desire to see a good thing spread.

Once a good thing is on the road to permanence, organizers are inevitably infected with an itch to see it expand.

Altruism is a seed of expansion. If something works, who would deny its benefits to the rest of mankind? Having struggled to organize a successful Garden Club, its members cannot resist the demands for help and advice from people who have yet to nurse their own clubs beyond survival. These pleas cannot be ignored.

This is the *Expansion Trap*:

If Something Is Good, It Should Expand; To Make It Expand, Organize It.

How It Is Done

Both the Organizing Trap and the Expansion Trap are baited by the same two-step process.

(1) Divide the labor.

(2) Establish a hierarchy.

Division of labor is recognition of the proverbial truth that too many cooks spoil the broth, all the more so if they are zealous cooks. Harnessing enthusiasm demands that a job be split into specialties. With each specialist toiling in an exclusive domain, individual efficiency goes up and the efficiency of the whole system goes way up.

If efficiency were not reason enough, division of labor also drives out despised uncertainty. Action becomes predictable; people become accountable. Whistlehalt publicity is no longer left to whimsy or good fortune, but to Barkdale. Because publicity is Barkdale's only task, soon enough he learns to do it quite well and without wasted effort. Division of labor has made him efficient.

Dividing the labor is, however, only half the task. A stable of specialists milling about is little more than a technically efficient anarchy. Still missing is a way to direct these specialized energies toward some common end. A boss is needed. Ergo, hierarchy appears in the first halting steps to save or expand a good thing. To avoid hierarchy is to leave things to chance. Nothing will be left to chance.

After such a bright beginning, it was inevitable that the founders of the Whistlehalt Obedience Club would organize and organize again. We have seen how Barkdale took charge of publicity. Other divisions of labor followed. Pinchbuck became treasurer. The job of scouting training sites went to Dr. Strainleash. To coordinate and control these busy specialists, Dogwood accepted the club's presidency. He chose Arfman as vice-president and director of training operations. A hierarchy was born.

Today the Whistlehalt Obedience Club boasts an executive vice-president, three vice-presidents, a swarm of committee heads, and a host of project directors. This is the consequence of the noble idea that no puppy should be deprived of training for want of a group rate.

Together, division of labor and hierarchy assure the survival and expansion of a good thing, whether a fast-food stand or a political movement.

The Traps Observed

Having learned of the Organizing Trap and the Expansion Trap, no one should be surprised to read that mantra-chanting Hare Krishnas hawked their scented lotions and candles to the tune of $30 million a year. Such success was not the result of meditation alone; there was a tight sales plan supervised by the cult's national marketing director.

Go paddle a canoe? Not by yourself. "Too dangerous," says an official of the United States Canoe Association. "To enjoy something, it has to be organized." Of course. Few could leave canoeing safety to chance. On the contrary, safety must be in the specialized hands of a safety chairman.

However absurd it is to find that street musicians in San Francisco must be licensed, the city supervisors acted from pure intentions. To perpetuate the public's delight in street music, the supervisors had to regulate this spontaneous entertainment. Some of these merchants of melody might be muggers or, worse still, incompetent artists. Who dares leave such things to chance?

Getting Away from It All

Fleeing a bureaucratized world requires the use of the very principles underlying bureaucracy. Witness the get-away-from-it-all retreat of Eliot and Sue Coleman to a farm in Maine. Four years after running from an over-commercialized society, the Colemans were promoting the sale of their organically grown produce through newspaper advertisements, roadside signs, giveaway recipes, and bonuses of fresh flowers. Eliot, sensing that their original goal had been compromised, admitted to the *Wall Street Journal*, "I feel in a way I've blown it here and I've let the place get too big."

Yet, if it were to survive at all, their adventure could not have turned out any other way. They started a good thing. To survive, it had to be organized. Survival conquered, expansion inevitably followed. Any other way of making a living from organic farming would have left too much to chance.

To Escape a Bureaucracy You Need a Bureaucracy

Consider the fate of the Sierra Survival Association, which began when three San Francisco executives tried to escape their regimented lives by fleeing to the remote Sierras. These visionaries had one inescapable problem: none of them knew a jot about surviving in a wilderness.

They quickly realized that survival requires a community of specialists. One to find a retreat site. Another to plan physical security. Others to oversee construction, sanitation, medical care, education of children, and entertainment. Unless retreating is done correctly, it should not be done at all. The first requirement is a division of labor.

Dividing the labor in the Association demanded a larger group. That alone compelled the addition of still another specialty: recruiting new members.

Where work is specialized, hierarchy must follow. It can be no other way. To resist hierarchy is to imperil a good thing.

And so it was that the Association survived. Today it has three layers of hierarchy presiding over an army of specialists. It had also changed its name to High Sierra Development, Inc., a firm that sells get-away-from-it-all condominiums.

You cannot escape a bureaucratized world without building a bureaucracy to do it. Anything else leaves too much to chance.

The Joy of Bureaucracy

In the beginning—long before a good thing has swelled into a top-heavy hierarchy—the benefits of the first organizing steps are irresistible. No one can resist what works so well. But once begun, there is no end to it. Bureaucracy is inevitable because its benefits are irresistible.

Many will object that the Whistlehalt Obedience Club, the Coleman farm, and the Sierra Survival Association are not what they have in mind when complaining of "bureaucracy." True, but this is precisely why the illustrations used here are not drawn from the case files about giant bureaucracies. The lesson is that all organizational giants have sprung from warm little groups doing good things.

A Simple Past

Formalization was not always the fate of civilized people. On the contrary.

In past decades mothers stole time for themselves by foisting their offspring on grandparents.

Once upon a time college newspapers were written and managed entirely by part-time student volunteers.

Before computers and big-project science, scholars required scarcely any funding beyond their teaching salaries and an occasional sabbatical leave.

Years ago shortwave radio hobbyists tuned in distant broadcasts unassisted by the incentives of national awards or the consolation of radio-club chaplains.

Tennis buffs of yore did little more about their avocation than play tennis. Editing a tennis-club newsletter—instead of lobbing and smashing—would have struck them as missing the point.

Spontaneity Is Doomed

Bureaucracy will prevail. Everything is becoming more organized, more formal, more regulated. With each passing year there are more forms to complete, more meetings to attend, more schedules to arrange, and more justifications to write for what is already being done. Production and pleasure are being replaced by control and compliance. Spontaneity is doomed.

To those still provoked to ask what can be done to save spontaneity, the only answer is: "Nothing." To ask how to stem the relentless flood of formality is to ask how to suppress altruism, the noble wellspring of the Organizing Trap and the Expansion Trap. Bureaucracy is founded not on vices but on virtues.

We Are All Bureaucracy Junkies

Bureaucracy, in truth, is not a monster run amok; it is not a party-crasher. On the contrary, it enters only where invited. So attractive are the early benefits of organizing that its eventual victims are the first to seek its wonders. People everywhere are busy setting up committees, calling meetings, creating departments, writing rules, promulgating procedures, and scheduling their lives down to the minute. A craving for controls beats in the collective heart of mankind. While all resent the over-organization imposed upon themselves, they nevertheless—in all innocence and with good intentions—impose it on others.

Each sees "bureaucracy" as something fashioned by others. Organizations *we* create are never "bureaucracies"; they are instruments in our struggle "to get things done."

Chapter 3

Bureaucracy Begins at Home

Why We Wouldn't Have It Any Other Way

The fault, dear Brutus, is not in our stars,
But in ourselves, that we are underlings.
—Julius Caesar

Routinization is coming to dominate every facet of our lives.

What a Difference a Steam Engine Makes

The world wasn't always this way. Hunting and gathering societies—our own primitive ancestors—didn't know about formal organizations. A caveman hunted with his kinsmen so that the entire band could eat. The medieval artisan ran his shop, and the pioneer settler his farm, in much the same way. But then came the steam engine with its capacity to produce more goods than the kinship system could handle.

A new form of organization was needed to match the power of the steam engine. That new form was the formal authority hierarchy.

A modern automobile can only be built by a bureaucratic organization. Agriculture on the scale needed to feed the world's population requires bureaucracy. Few of us would accept the low productivity and social oppression of tight little communities toiling at their crafts and trying to eke subsistence from the soil.

Bureaucracy exists because we need what it can do. Not only do we need it but we *want* it.

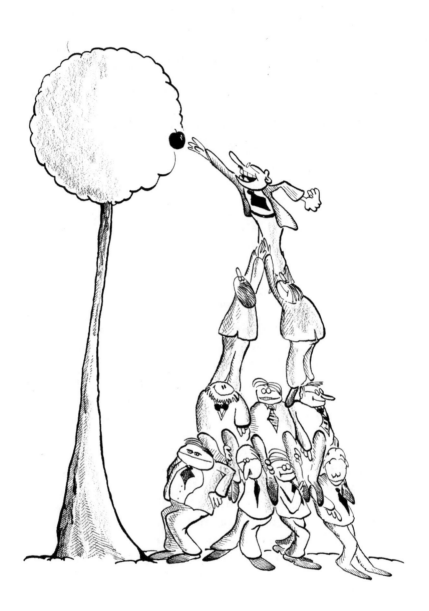

Double Your Pleasure

Once upon a time kids shot aggies on vacant lots; today there is a National Marble Championship with elaborate eligibility requirements and local and regional elimination rounds. Playing marbles becomes serious business if you can win trophies in Atlantic City.

A few years ago skateboard enthusiasts attached old roller-skate wheels to boards and zipped along the streets; today there are formal skate parks complete with pro shops. Why should a skateboarder be content navigating Main Street when he can test himself against the undulations of a track approved by the American Skateboard Association?

Surfing, that symbol of spontaneous fun, now has an American Surfing Association to standardize its practice and promote its acceptance as an Olympic sport. Submitting to the rigors of the Bonzai Pipeline takes on added significance when it can earn a surfer a crack at the Surfing Hall of Fame.

Every year more of the fun things in life fall under the domain of formal systems because we want it that way.

If you rent a horse in Connecticut, insurance regulations require you to ride in the company of a stable hand. Protest as you may, you either ride with the stable hand or you don't ride at all. On second thought you realize that riding without insurance coverage would be leaving things to chance. Nothing will be left to chance.

There is no conspiracy by sinister forces to spoil carefree pursuits. There is no plot to eliminate all free-form enjoyment. On the contrary, each and every one of us is a partner in the gradual disappearance of spontaneity. Bureaucracy is the work of everyman.

Do It to Me Again

In man's desperation to quash doubt, he will always choose organization over spontaneity.

Hikers, despite a desire to spend their unprogrammed hours in solitude, invariably join the Sierra Club, a beneficent bureaucracy but a bureaucracy nonetheless. Without the Sierra Club hikers couldn't gain access to private ranchland trails. They could always take off on their own down U.S. government Wilderness Trails, but without an experienced guide and a certified practitioner of mountain rescue techniques, the risk would be forbidding. For hikers, the path of least resistance leads to the Sierra Club.

Organizing is our natural answer to risk. It matters not that organizing works best in the beginning. It matters not that it is addictive. It matters not that what was born of innocent intentions may become uncontrollable. All we ever see are the early benefits. All we ever see is that a system gives us what we want.

Matters of National Importance

The Special Prosecutor's Office had a decisive impact on the Watergate scandal. As an ad hoc appointee, the special prosecutor was outside the Justice Department's organization chart but he got the job done.

The only problem was that the President who was being investigated had to create and fill the office. Can we trust Presidents to do the right thing? What would happen if a scandal broke and the President didn't act? Can we allow the government to leave something as obviously effective as the special prosecutor to caprice?

Decidedly not. Congress established the Office of Government Crimes, freezing the virtues of the temporary, informal Special Prosecutor's Office into a permanent bureau.

Few would object to the creation of a permanent Office of Government Crimes. It gave the public the reassurance it craved. It matters not that the occasional cynic would besmirch this step as rank bureaucratic action.

An Apparent Exception

Some may deny Haga's Law, arguing that apparent exceptions to it abound. Work and play, they might assert, are undertaken all the time—among close friends, long-time employees, or kinfolk—without a hint of permanent organization. Thousands of entrepreneurial families, the doubters will point out, run small businesses without resort to division of labor or hierarchy.

Haga's Law implies that such delightful endeavors are the exception now and will be more so in the future. No large, complicated enterprise can be managed successfully with only friendship or kinship as a guide. In a society anxiously beating back the demon of chance, kinship and trust are inadequate for the drive to get things done.

Bureaucracy Begins at Home

We all prefer organizing because we all want to get things done. Those who claim they abhor officialdom and hierarchy are only claiming that they prefer anxiety to certainty. In fact, we condemn bureaucracy only when it is abstract or remote. Confronted by concrete threats, faced with work to be done, we organize.

Drawing the Line

While all are quick to endorse freedom, an undeniable benefit of authority hierarchies—for each of us—is that they keep a leash on others. We can't leave to the judgment of an ambitious Little League manager how often his star left-hander will pitch. He might play the boy too often and injure his arm. There must be a rule limiting the number of innings a boy may pitch.

If we must limit the discretion of managers in Little

League, can we permit it to clerks in a welfare office? Can we trust the impulses of even the most honest functionaries not to favor some clients while indulging personal distastes in denying others? No, only neutral rules—not the whims of well-intentioned civil servants—can be trusted to draw the line.

Few would want policemen to wield their pistols without thought. However much it might inhibit the pursuit of felons, we feel safer knowing that regulations require law officers to render a detailed accounting, to a board of inquiry, for every bullet fired. Who would want it any other way?

Clearly, no one could live with the uncertainty of leaving to a Strategic Air Command pilot the decision to launch a nuclear attack. Certainty requires a chain of command leading up to ultimate civilian control. Is this a bureaucracy any reasonable citizen would want to eschew?

The benefits of organizing are beyond serious question. Organizing prevails because we want the things it does for us. But organizing means making rules. And, as even pedestrian observers have noted, rules always become holy decrees. Finally, nothing, not even your own personal, special case will be left to chance. Thus does bureaucracy get in the way. There is no alternative.

Thus another paradox: Mankind has two qualms about bureaucracies: first that they will come to be, and second that they won't.

Chapter 4

The Potato Chip Imperative

Why a Hierarchy Can't Quit While It's Ahead

Can we ever have too much of a good thing?
—Miguel de Cervantes

Organizations always go too far.

Observing how well a little arranging and standardizing can reduce uncertainty, people in a new organization are invariably driven to systemize still more. Once the fall begins, the decline is swift.

It happens every day.

Spinnaker, who lives four and a half minutes from the Through Channels Sailing Club, resigned his membership. He has his afternoons free and loves sailing, but he couldn't endure the paperwork. A club boat had to be reserved six days in advance, each cruise was limited to ninety minutes on Regiment Bay, and the club rules mandated that a skipper and mate—trained and certified by the club—be aboard. The club had taken the fun out of sailing. Official procedure must dominate even leisure pursuits.

Roscoe, the Rembrandt of advertising art directors, lost his job at a hot little ad agency when it folded. Only in its third year of business, this outfit died from an overdose of cost controls. Formality prevailed over purpose. Every ten minutes each employee in the agency had to write down what he or she was doing. It wasn't fun to work there any-

more. The sharpest creative people left for other jobs. Then the agency lost its clients.

In testifying before the US Commission on Federal Paperwork, a spokesman for the American Bankers Association announced that the ABA had kept its statement on the wonders of reducing paperwork to a single page. However, the press release that summarized the one-page statement ran to two pages. The ABA could not stop while it was ahead.

Captains of US naval ships have had some twenty duties added to their jobs since World War II. During the Vietnam conflict, many officers wondered whether they were losing men and weapons because of ambiguous administrative demands. Many commanding officers were paperwork-weary, rather than battle-weary, from trying to do too much and still do it all well. The Navy hierarchy had gone too far.

With barely seven days to prepare, Israeli commandos executed a nearly perfect rescue of hostages from Entebbe Airport. A similar raid by American forces to grab fifty-five POWs out of Son Tay prison camp near Hanoi consumed fourteen months of preparation and 170 rehearsals. When the U.S. assault team finally landed, the Son Tay camp was empty.

Once a spontaneous, informal endeavor gets under way, the natural forces of Haga's Law propel it toward over-organization. The fear of leaving anything to chance drives otherwise humane people into going too far.

Demise of the Yellow Card

Doris Grumbach recalls, for the *Chronicle of Higher Education,* that when she taught at a small Catholic women's college of 1,200 students, there were only three administrators. One of them, Sister Clare, the registrar, kept track of students, course enrollments, and grades with a simple system of yellow cards. The efficient sister is gone now, replaced by an administrative computer housed in three air-conditioned rooms and tended by four people. In the meantime, the college's enrollment is still not much more than 1,200.

In contrast to the days of the yellow card, faculty and students at administratively sophisticated schools are now assaulted at the beginning of each semester by as many as five mailings of computerized class rosters and Student Status Reports before registration is "finalized."

Jock Bureaucracy

Runaway organizing has long been as common in the sports world as athlete's foot. Hierarchy and careerism have overrun fun and fitness. In the early days of scholastic games, students got together on their own time to compete in "club" sports. They elected a team captain. Soon enough the captain hired a coach. Part-time coaches became full-time coaches. The clubs were institutionalized into an Athletic Association.

Once started, the organizing addiction could not stop. Full-time coaches became head coaches, supervising a covey of lesser coaches, trainers, equipment managers, and water boys. This growing core was further fattened with sports publicists, orthopedic physicians, and grounds crews. There is no end to it.

The Fallacy

Authorities on bureaucratic processes have long recognized that the urge to over-organize is actually a specific case of the more general human propensity, the *Linear Escalation Fallacy*. In its modern scientific expression the Fallacy predicts that if a little bit does a little good, a whole lot is bound to do wonders.*

Applied to organizing, the Linear Escalation Fallacy seduces otherwise reasonable minds. The smallest dose of organizing does get rid of a lot of uncertainty. Moreover, a touch of organizing yields efficiencies not possible when things are done spontaneously. The cheese having been bitten, the Organizing Trap is sprung. The Fallacy dictates that a whole lot more organizing is bound to eliminate *all* surprises and render every scheme marvelously efficient. Figure 2 depicts the world as addicted organizers see it.

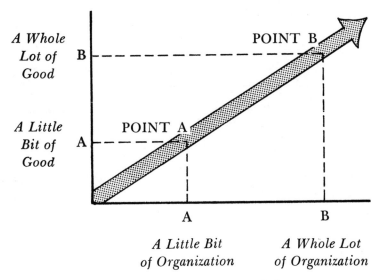

Figure 2. The Linear Escalation Fallacy

* The ancient Fallacy was revealed to me by my sainted father, who unswervingly used linear escalation as a guide to applying fertilizer to lawn and garden. That linear escalation was, in practice, a fallacy became clear to me on the evidence of the perennially burnt grass and wilted flora that were the consequence of a "whole lot more" fertilizer.—W.J.H.

Diminishing Returns

Reality, however, rarely conforms to linear logic. The fruit of more and more organizing does not plot on a graph as a straight line rising forever unimpeded.

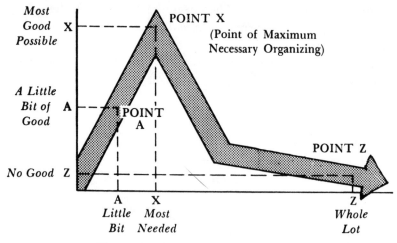

Figure 3. The Inverted V Reality

Figure 3 reveals that a little bit of organizing does create a little bit of good. A little bit *more* actually causes things to get even better. But only up to a point, Point X to be exact.

Beyond Point X, however, more organizing leads not to more good but to less. That is precisely the point where more organizing becomes over-organizing. The downturn is what addicted organizers cannot see.

Forsooth, Figure 3 makes plain that precious little organizing yields all the good that can be squeezed from any organizing at all. All too soon a thriving system rushes past Point X on the Inverted V curve and plunges into the region of Diminishing Returns. An organization that presses beyond Point X—toward a narrower division of labor, a taller hierarchy, or a fatter rule book—must finally collapse into terminal administrative dysfunction.

The Inverted V at Work

Few would deny that obedience training for big, unruly dogs would never have happened in Whistlehalt but for the collective logic of forming the Whistlehalt Obedience Club. Fewer still could foresee that the club would *not* stop organizing itself once it had its original purpose—dog training —well within grasp.

Dogwood mercifully gaveled a recent business meeting into adjournment at 1:15 A.M. The session had begun at 7:30 P.M. and quickly bogged down in debate over the choice of official club colors, with the powerful German Shepherd bloc holding out for black and brown.

The Cozy Co-op also reaped the early benefits of a little organizing. It reduced the cost of housing and created equity for all eight owners—within a framework that gave everyone a voice in managing the investment. But good things have a way of getting out of hand. One member was habitually late with his rent. Another neglected janitorial duties. The only conceivable solution—even for a group of eight—was to organize still more. The president appointed an assistant treasurer, who would dun tardy shareholders for the rent. The board of directors devised check-off forms for janitorial duties and required weekly reports to a new vice-president for maintenance. The secretary chaired a special committee to promulgate penalties for dilatory members. Say hello to Point Z.

The learned Professor Schvitzmaven, father of preventive sociology, has confessed to us that his creative energies, once devoted solely to research, are now dissipated in administering it: writing proposals for funding, politicking with foundation executives, preparing interim progress reports, and concocting annual justifications for monies spent. Once a prolific scholar, Schvitzmaven has not produced a finding in years. He is too busy managing projects to do any research. Funding agencies that were originally supposed to foster basic research now unwittingly hinder it. They have gone too far.

The Potato Chip Imperative Made Me Do It

Our analysis of innumerable case studies discloses that organizations go too far precisely because organizers are without a clue as to the actual whereabouts of Point X. Managers can—and usually do—pass the Point of Maximum Necessary Organization without knowing it. In practice, organizers can sense the existence of Point X only after they are *well* past it, somewhere in the vicinity of Point Z. By then it is too late. By the time a system has slipped toward Point Z, there is no turning back in quest of the elusive optimum X.

Why, since reality evidently adheres to the Inverted V curve, do rational people, with rare exception, persist in acting as if the Linear Escalation Fallacy were true? It is akin to a group of errant navigators who, upon seeing satellite photos of Earth, stiffen their belief that the planet is flat. Our long and serious consideration of the evidence obliges us to conclude that the human mind, as organizer of work and play, is a slave to the *Potato Chip Imperative*:

Having Tasted the Benefits of a Little Bit of Organizing, No One Can Resist the Temptation to Organize a Little Bit More.

Familiar Workings

The psychological workings of the Imperative are well known to potato chip fanciers. Delighted by the taste of a first potato chip, no one can resist a second. A second leads irresistably to a third. With a third, all restraint erodes and the victim falls to gobbling every chip in the bowl, eventually using both hands to hurry the desperate process.

As it is with potato chips, so it is with organizing.

A little bit of organizing is the first potato chip on the road to over-organization.

Pooling funds to do together what no one can do alone is a first potato chip. Electing a treasurer to handle the pooled funds is a second chip.

Making specific work assignments is a first potato chip. Holding people accountable for results is a second.

When things go so well after the first potato chip, only a fool would forgo the second or refuse the third. Before long, nothing will be left to chance.

Chapter 5

The Quicksand Corollary

Nothing Flails Like Excess

Whoso diggeth a pit shall fall therein.
—Proverbs 26:27

The more a bureaucracy tries to climb out of the mire of over-organization, the deeper it sinks.

The Potato Chip Imperative (which dictates that once organizing starts, it cannot stop) explains well enough how small organizations are seduced into over-organizing. But the Imperative is inadequate to explain how overgrown, calcified systems, already sinking into the quagmire of over-organization, work themselves into ever deeper trouble. The Imperative cannot explain why the Post Office, unable to move the mail with a five-digit ZIP code, claims the solution lies with nine digits.

To understand this phenomenon we must postulate the *Quicksand Corollary*:

Every Effort to Fix Bureaucracy Invariably Makes It Worse.

Evidence Abounds

New York Hospital in Manhattan became so burdened with procedures that it lapsed into ineptitude. The hospital director met this problem as administrators far and wide meet problems, with still more organizing. Having discovered that the person who was losing out was the patient, the director created an Office of Patient Representatives. When

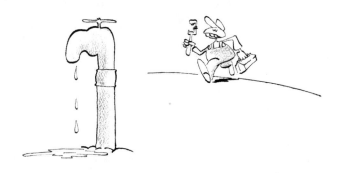

a system doesn't work, it adds another layer of hierarchy.

A study of the national bureaucracy of a major Protestant denomination revealed that an earlier reorganization had concentrated on *how* work was being done, ignoring *what* the final purposes of this vast system were. The church's decision makers then combined agencies and departments into fewer, but bigger, superbureaus. This step served only to hamper communication and blur lines of authority. When something is too big, it gets bigger.

Former Secretary of Health, Education and Welfare Joseph Califano, anxious to be in the vanguard of President Carter's crusade against bureaucracy, launched "Operation Common Sense" to reduce the number of his ministry's regulations and make them easier to read. HEW publicists heralded this blow to paperwork with a press release forty-three pages long. The centerpiece of "Operation Common Sense" was the creation of one more sub-cabinet post, the Deputy General Counsel for Regulatory Review. When something is complex, another official is added to simplify it.

Why Systems Cannot De-organize

Only the naïve expect the difficulties of over-organization to be solved by less organization, by de-organizing. It is the rare corporate chairman—or even garden-club president—who knows the first thing about de-organizing. It is not a technique taught in graduate business schools, which have no interest in less organizing, only in more. No de-organizing courses exist in MBA curricula, because, in truth, de-organizing is metaphysically impossible. De-organizing would move a system toward uncertainty, push it in the direction of leaving some things to chance, force it to violate Haga's Law. Systems always move in the direction of *more* certainty. Nothing will be left to chance.

From HEW down to the Junior League the only thing managers know is how to organize. When over-organization rears its head, managers never recognize it for what it is. On the contrary, over-organization always appears in the guise of a problem, which managers attempt to solve by the only means they know.* Organizing! It worked in the past; it will work again.

When the members of the Cozy Co-op finally found themselves tangled in the duties of running their apartment building, they cast about for a solution. They did not cast far. Having succeeded in organizing away their initial problems, they organized once again. They created the full-time post of building superintendent and engaged a managing agent. Thus did they nullify their earlier benefits of a little organizing without actually solving their current problems.

President Nixon's efforts to reorganize the federal bureaucracy led to the creation of not fewer but more agencies in the executive branch. Nixon's administration added fifty-three bureaus during his first term and twenty-three more in the first year of his second term.

President Carter came into office promising to streamline the government. He established a system whereby suggestions for pruning the bureaucracy could reach him only through the Office of the Domestic Policy Assistant. But the DPA first had to circulate an IDM (Issue Definition Memorandum). From the IDM, the DPA staff had to develop RM's (Response Memoranda) to discuss all know options. The staff then had to boil down the RM options into a PDM (Presidential Decision Memorandum). Any suggestion that survived all this would become a DPD (Domestic Presidential Directive).

---

* The single exception is that class of managers who, when faced with a problem, possess the virtue of being paralyzed into inaction.

They Never Learn

The earliest recorded example of the Quicksand Corollary was the French King Henry II's efforts to control the upstart nobility by sending *intendants* into the provinces to represent the crown in judicial and fiscal matters. These *intendants* inevitably succumbed to local influences and became unmanageable. To keep an eye on the *intendants,* the king created *commissionaires.* Soon enough the *commissionaires* also settled in. They, too, became part of the very system they were supposed to watch.*

President Carter, having forgotten French history, seems doomed to repeat it. In response to dismay over public mismanagement, Carter created twelve inspectors general to seek out fraud and negligence. These modern *commissionaires* will audit departments and investigate wrongdoing, already audited and investigated by the *intendants* of the General Accounting Office.

Zero-Based Bloating

A recent, devastating illustration of the Quicksand Corollary was the Federal government's much ballyhooed proposal for zero-based budgeting.

Everyone rejoiced to hear of this diet for the bloated bureaucracy. This, it seemed, was a serious challenge to the Quicksand Corollary. Early returns, however, showed the immutability of the Corollary. Instead of cutting bureaucracy down to size, zero-based budgeting actually made it larger.

Last year, for example, the Agency for Aardvark Resources Management (AARM) learned that it was due for a top-to-bottom zero-based review of every penny it was spending.

---

* From Henry Jacoby, *The Bureaucratization of The World.* Berkeley: University of California Press, 1973.

The news chilled Stackpaper, deputy assistant undersecretary for Aardvark Affairs. All the agency's time was already consumed in preparing overhead projector slides to sell AARM's latest proposal, the Center for Unicorn Preservation, to Congress. Obviously no one had a minute to spare for a justification of the *whole* AARM budget.

Stackpaper responded in the only way possible. He created a new office, the Special Assistant for Legislative Communication (SALC). SALC's mission was to impress Congress with AARM's contribution to the public interest.

The new SALC staff went on the offensive. Soon enough SALC employed 110 specialists in publicity, audio-visual presentation, and statistical manipulation. These professionals were supported by a multitude of secretaries, file clerks, accountants, illustrators, and speech writers. If Congress wanted to look at the whole AARM budget, then, by God, they would see it. Indeed, SALC would dazzle and numb the legislators with its presentation of AARM's place in the public weal. The mere threat of a zero-based review had stimulated further expansion of AARM's staff and budget.

Multiply this result by the hundreds of Stackpapers throughout the government. The result, undreamed of by well-intentioned reformers, has not been bureaucratic demise but organizational giantism. It cannot be any other way.

Solving the Insoluble

One reason so many organizations fall victim to the Quicksand Corollary is that enterprising managers cannot admit that some problems are beyond solution. The very nature of their jobs dictates that they do something about *every* problem. And once having done something about a problem, without having solved it, they must do something more. Caught in this counterproductive cycle of frustration, an organization quickly finds itself sinking in quicksand.

General Motors, once it learned of the existence of "blue-collar blues," had to do something about it. Unable to accept the fact that nothing will relieve the tedium of an assembly line, GM created a staff to deal with it. Even though GM already had an Industrial Relations Department to communicate with its employees, the company nevertheless added a new Personnel Development Department to probe the problems of blue-collar workers. When you can't solve a problem, double your staff.

The fuel shortage of 1973 offered another opportunity for a Quicksand solution. The shortage was caused by Middle Eastern politics, a complex knot well beyond the power of the U.S. government. Nevertheless, the government aggregated all known agencies, bureaus, and offices already dealing with energy into a new Cabinet-level Department of Energy, a mega-bureaucracy to attempt what its component bureaus could not do. By the time the new Department came into existence, however, the problem had passed, leaving behind an entity designed to work on a problem that no longer existed.

When trouble in the Middle East choked the supply of crude oil again in 1979, government misallocations of gasoline to retail stations only made matters worse, sparking panic at the pumps. The government attacked these bitter fruits of its own over-organizing by organizing still more. The mischief of the Department of Energy was bolstered with three new agencies: the Energy Security Corporation, the Energy Mobilization Board, and the Solar Bank.

Just a Step at a Time

To understand the nature of bureaucracy, we have to understand that no one *wants* over-organization.

As a matter of fact, *everyone* is against it. And yet we

encounter over-organization at every turn. Why? Because the process is unintentional and nearly invisible. Over-organization doesn't go down in great gulps, but in pecking little bites. It is dangerously incremental.

A corporation director or a Cabinet minister rarely faces a decision about the totality of his dominion. Decisions are made on the margin, not on the total.

The flow of illegal drugs across the Mexican-U.S. border is a source of concern for both governments. In Arizona there are a variety of law enforcement agencies working on the problem. Local police departments, the U.S. border patrol, federal customs officials, and the Arizona department of public safety all try to intercept heroin and opium coming from the Mexican state of Sonora. All this police power has shown itself incapable of stopping the flow of drugs. Therefore, a Four County Narcotics Strike Force was created to patrol the border. This too failed to halt the drug traffic. The state legislature, unaware of the Quicksand Corollary, decided that a statewide Drug Strike Force was the answer.

Over-organizing is inescapable. Every manager who falls into the mire of diminishing returns can only try to climb out by organizing still more. Because organizing has always worked before, managers will resort to a little hair of the organizational dog that bit them. Then, they will sit back and smile until the dog strikes again.

A Little Dab'll Do Ya In

Haga's Law dictates that uncertainties must be organized away. The mischief of over-organizing grows from the same root that gives rise to organizing in the first place, the dread of uncertainty. The early delight we take in overcoming a measure of unpredictability inevitably compels us to eradicate the last whisper of chance.

That's how the Quicksand Corollary draws a system deeper

into trouble. Few things are dangerous in tiny doses. Alcohol, marijuana, and even Louisiana red hot tabasco sauce are fine in small amounts. Likewise, organizing in moderation isn't evil. A little organizing helps. It preserves a good cause, spreads benefits, cuts costs, and erases uncertainty. But the system has to have more.

Even if a going concern set out to de-organize, it certainly would not proceed to do it willy-nilly. Hardly. It would set up a De-Organization Priorities Coordinating Task Force. Nothing must be left to chance.

Chapter 6

Scoreboard Bureaucracy

Blow in My Feedback Loop and I'll Follow You Anywhere

"Not men but measures": A sort of charm by which many people get loose from honourable engagement.

—Edmund Burke

Some organizations get money by selling things. Such systems are known as Demand Loops. Businesses as small as a roadside fruit stand and as large as Exxon provide things that outsiders want enough to pay for them. If a Demand Loop doesn't sell things, it doesn't get money to buy resources. No resources, no organization. As they have sown, so shall they reap.

All other organizations are Breakloops. These systems get resources in one of two ways. Some take gifts; others steal. Breakloops can, therefore, reap without sowing.

How Demand Loops Work

The litmus test of Demand Loop survival is performance.

If the roadside fruit stand provides fresh peaches and apples, customers will come back.

Exxon works the same way, at least in theory.

The scoreboard for Demand Loops is the bottom line.

Figure 4. How Demand Loop Systems Work

How Breakloops Work

Breakloops, by comparison, must look elsewhere for indicators of how how well they are doing. They must find surrogate scoreboards.

Figure 5.   How Breakloop Systems Work

Paying and Using

The distinguishing feature of Demand Loops is that the people who use them are the same people who pay for them. Such is not the case for Breakloops.

The closest connection between paying and using in a Breakloop arises when homeowner Miremazel occasionally approves of his local government—and even that connection is crimped. Property taxes in Regiment City pay for the resources that the public schools and the fire and police departments consume. Miremazel feels protected by the police and fire departments and sends his children to Regiment City's schools. Isn't he a user as well as a payer? It seems so. But the reality is otherwise. Miremazel can't buy services from Regiment City in use-by-use, dollar-for-dollar transactions. The choice is not his to purchase police protection while declining the services of the fire department. When his children have grown and gone, he still pays for the school system.

Miremazel's taxpaying is, therefore, not connected with his use of government. There is no link between what a Breakloop does and how it acquires the money to keep doing it. Lacking a feedback loop, it has no choice but to extort or accept alms. Civics textbook rhetoric aside, what a government does is mug the governed. Governments make us "pay or else"; that is the difference between Manny's Delicatessen and the Post Office.

At the state and national level there is not even the illusion of a connection between paying and using. While many citizens will argue that they want national defense, they do not use it directly. Indeed, they are scarcely aware of it at all—unless there is an invasion. Organizations for which everyone pays and which everyone uses anonymously are prototypical Breakloops. They are the most likely candidates for bureaucratization.

Alms Springs

Other Breakloops, the whole panoply of nonprofit institutions and charities, get their money from gifts. They may be beggars and not thieves, but they suffer from the same disconnection between who pays and who benefits. While people donate money or volunteer labor to charities, hospitals, religious groups, and legal defense funds for a variety of emotional, moral, and tax-deductible reasons, these donations carry no expectation of pecuniary return.

Vagrant Influences

Demand Loops possess two virtues Breakloops lack, virtues that dampen the urge to bureaucratize.

• Demand Loops know, by and large, *what* they are doing. General Motors realizes it makes cars.

• Demand Loops can also approximate how much the outside world *cares* about what they are doing. They have a clear scoreboard linking them to their users in the environment. Manny's Delicatessen can measure its success or failure in sales or profits.

Lacking this kind of scoreboard, Breakloop organizations face one of two dilemmas.

• Some Breakloops can't decide what they do. This leaves them susceptible to vagrant influences. A number of American state universities never knew what they wanted to be. So they tried to be everything and nearly went out of business in the effort.

• Other Breakloops are deliberate about what they are, but the *worth* of their outputs is unknowable. People who borrow books from a public library know it is useful; they have the books to prove it. But the patrons can't put a dollar value on a library's usefulness. As a result, librarians cannot calculate the worth of libraries, only the costs.

Closet Breakloops

Within Demand Loop systems there are unsuspected nests of Breakloops.

A corporation's public-relations department is a parasitic Breakloop leeching off its host Demand Loop. Consider Lockstep Bootery. Essentially it *donates* an annual budget to its PR department. No one thinks of the PR budget as a donation, but that's exactly what it is.

Lockstep is undeniably the payer for its PR, but it is not so obviously the user. Lockstep's executives simply have no way of determining whether the PR they buy has any effect on corporate performance any more than there is a way of measuring whether a definitive Breakloop such as the Department of Health, Education and Welfare leaves us healthy, wealthy, or wise. While a PR department looks like a Demand Loop branch, it is actually a hidden Breakloop.

Reaping without Sowing

When an organization can get its hands on resources without selling any output, it need not worry about the quality—or even the existence—of what it does. If an organization can reap without sowing, why should it sow? Since Breakloops lack feedback connections, we have no way of making them listen. We can neither reward them for the good they do nor punish them for the bad. Therefore, Breakloops are notoriously hard of hearing.

Some Breakloops we love, such as San Francisco's cable cars, but that does not keep them from the brink of demise. Others we fear, such as the Revenue Service, but that does not stop their growing power. Still others we may ignore, such as the United Nations. And a few we hardly know exist, such as the International Monetary Fund. But whatever our attitude toward them, it affects them not one whit.

See How They Reap

Postal workers get paid no matter how slowly they handle the mail.

Superintendents of education and their hordes of counselors and coordinators will get paid despite a growing rate of illiteracy. Indeed, the education establishment invariably seizes upon the growth of illiteracy to justify additional funds to redouble its futile efforts.

The trustees of a volunteer agency cannot measure the value of its community programs, but their ambitious executive director knows they can count. Accordingly, he doubles the number of the programs in the agency. While this saps the effectiveness of each program, the board will commend his administrative vigor, raise his salary, and increase the size of his staff.

It's Not the People

Breakloop systems can measure their costs, but they never know what their output is worth, what benefits they bring to others. In the final analysis it doesn't matter. Breakloop systems will get their hands on resources again and again whether their people do good work, poor work, or no work at all.

Ask a PR man about his output. He will talk about his eighty-three press releases per month, his fifteen speeches a quarter, and his two annual meetings. That isn't output; that's input. Keep pressing. Ask what the input does for his organization.

Talk to a social worker. What's his output? He will talk about his case load. But that's input. What is he accomplishing?

Or a university dean. Output? He'll tell you that his school will graduate four thousand students in June. Surprising as it may seem, that's not output.

The Flesh Is Weak

No worker in a Breakloop system has to worry that if he doesn't please the public his employer will die of resource starvation. A Demand Loop would soon enough collapse if it allowed rudeness or sloth. The difference is not in the individual personalities of Demand Loop and Breakloop workers. Breakloops have no demonic genius for finding uncivil, unresponsive people. It just seems that way. The difference is not in the temperaments of the workers but in the designs of their organizations. The flesh, after all, is weak. A Breakloop encourages that weakness.

Up from Edsel

That Breakloops couldn't care less about the world around them is scarcely surprising. The wonder is that we expect them to behave otherwise. They have no way of recognizing their mistakes and no motive to correct them.

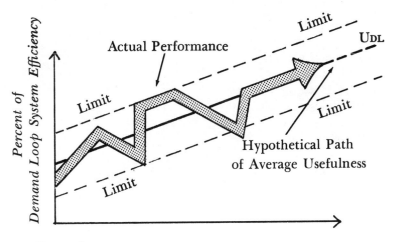

Figure 6.
Limits on Deviation of Demand Loop from Usefulness

Trained analysts can see from Figure 6 that the actual course taken by a Demand Loop system wanders from the Hypothetical Path of Average Usefulness (U_{DL}). It cannot wander far, however. Its mistakes and excesses are limited by how few organizational groceries it can buy from the environment if it isn't selling useful outputs.

In the mid-1950s the Ford Motor Company brought out the Edsel, a product that was out of step with the world from the day it was introduced. But while Edsel became a household synonym for "goof," Ford, because it is a Demand Loop, was compelled to correct its mistake.

Casting Errors in Bronze

No such constraints hinder the wanderings of a Breakloop system. Cut off from the outside world, Breakloops are damned to drift farther and farther out of phase with their environments. As Figure 7 makes clear, the actual path taken

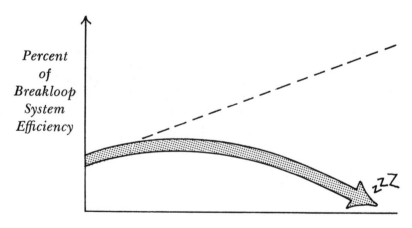

Figure 7.
No Limit on Breakloop Deviation from Usefulness

by a Breakloop can vary greatly from U_{BL}. Since it need not sell outputs to buy groceries, the Breakloop eats no matter how useless it becomes.

Breakloops are slow to respond. In the 1930s the French built the Maginot Line in anticipation of an invasion from Germany. Ineffective during World War II, the Maginot Line was maintained in spit-and-polish condition until 1966.

Immune from Punishment

A storm of public protest beating on a Breakloop's door may be the first inkling that something is amiss. The Post Office, for example, has no impetus to change its letter-by-letter sorting techniques. No one can reward it for improving or punish it for stagnating. The public is compelled to use the Post Office, whose public subsidy is the break in its feedback loop. If we try to punish the Post Office by sending fewer letters or by sending packages via United Parcel Service, the Post Office suffers not at all. It goes right on buying resources with the money it gets by extortion.

Innovating without Feedback

With old guard managers operating in a feedback vacuum, a Breakloop will do what it has always done while slowly drifting away from the Path of Usefulness. Things actually get worse, however, when bright, energetic managers take control. They always try to get the organization back on the Path of Usefulness (U_{BL}). The only way they can do this is by blindly tinkering. The inherent lack of feedback will prevent them from finding U_{BL}.

Public schools began as a commonsense idea. They seemed to work acceptably well—until concerned "educators" took the reins of the system. They tried new teaching techniques, not because the public demanded anything new but because they had no other way of seeking U_{BL}.

Being well schooled, these administrators knew that the environment changes constantly, however imperceptibly. To avoid the road to uselessness, they tried being innovative.

But, lacking a feedback loop, not even the best and brightest could find the Hypothetical Path of Usefulness (U_{BL}). They could only cast about—first here, then there— on a trial-and-error search for utility. (See Figure 8.)

The lesson for astute bureaucracy watchers is that Break-loops cannot improve under so-called professional managers. Compared to the smoothness of the old guard's decline into futility (Figure 7), the path taken by restless, public-spirited managers is erratic and equally futile. In their professional meanderings they only eat up more resources to get to the same place.

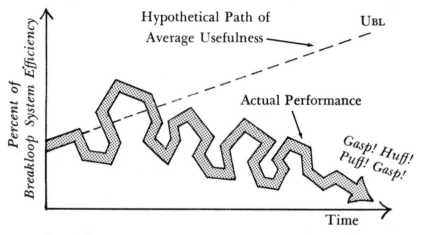

Figure 8.
Deviation of Breakloop from Usefulness when Run by Best and Brightest

Decisions in the Dark

While Breakloops and Demand Loops differ in their connection to the outside world, internally they must make the same kinds of decisions:

    1. to hire and fire people;

2. to promote, demote, and transfer people;
3. to accept or reject proposals for new things to do; and
4. to decide how big each department's slice of the budget pie will be.

On the inside, Ford Motor Company and the Post Office face identical administrative problems. But Ford Motor can make internal decisions according to the feedback it gets from the outside world. Ford can promote a foreman because he has a record of profitability based on low cost and high-quality output. The company can reward a salesman with bonuses for selling above quota. The firm can relate a secretary's work to the organization's goals and offer her advanced management schooling.

The Post Office, by contrast, can't readily make the same kinds of internal decisions using feedback from the external world. The Post Office isn't connected to the external world. The seniority system and civil-service examinations are the only criteria the Post Office has for making decisions about employees. Neither has much to do with the users of the Post Office.

Up against the Scoreboard

Since they cannot measure the usefulness their work has for outsiders, Breakloop managers concoct make-believe yardsticks of how well they are doing. These do not measure what anybody outside the system wants or would buy. They measure things that Breakloop decision makers can see and understand.

Military systems present a curious mix of Demand Loop and Breakloop behavior. In combat, armies have a starkly realistic scoreboard: battles won, territory gained, casualties suffered, and weapons destroyed.

Comes peace and those scoreboards disappear. The feed-back loop consequently unravels. The implacable wartime ship commander often becomes uneasy in the arena of peace-time gamesmanship. A brilliant tactician in combat, he is at a loss to finesse paperwork ashore. Another officer, indecisive or worse in combat, thrives when judged by such Breakloop criteria as the brilliance of his policy recommendations.

Peacetime promotions necessarily depend on surrogate scoreboards. Rarely does skill in ship driving contribute to a successful naval career in peacetime.

Naval officers might argue that brilliant memoranda and polished brass *are* important to combat readiness. But that contention is more folklore than fact. A private contractor for fire protection in Scottsdale, Arizona, has put to rest the myth that only shiny fire engines can help put out fires.

WIN
System Can Be Recognized for
Outstanding Performance

		YES	NO
LOSE System Can Be Recognized for Errors	**YES**	THE SHIFTSCHEME RESPONSE	THE BLUNDERFRET ADAPTATION
	NO	THE FIRECRACKER RESPONSE	THE TURNSTILE ADAPTATION

Figure 9.
Dichotomized Bivariate Analysis of Organizational Behavior

Surrogate Scoreboards

In Breakloop systems, managers have to make decisions; workers must arrange their tasks. Both, therefore, invent artificial scoreboards to measure achievement or guide daily endeavor. The salient dimensions of analyzing Breakloop behavior are *winning* and *losing*. Can a job or department garner gold stars? Can it avoid black marks? Can it do both? Or neither? A dichotomized bivariate analysis of organizations lacking feedback loops has led us to identify four Breakloop Behavior Types. Each type, to avoid its own uselessness, exhibits a unique form of surrogate scoreboard in response to Breakloop pressures. (See Figure 9.)

Chapter 7

The Shiftscheme Response

Do Something!

*He started to sing
as he tackled the thing
That couldn't be done.*
—Edgar A. Guest

Dog feces littered the sidewalks of Regiment City. Short of shooting the entire canine population, the problem was without genuine solution. Nevertheless, something had to be done. The chief public-health officer responded with a "do something" program: require people walking dogs to carry "pooper-scoopers" to clean up after their pets. Who could resist the common sense of such a solution?

Parents wrung their hands over the safety of their children who are away at camp. The Ministry of Public Concern, unable to shield each and every child from the perils of play, nevertheless did not hesitate to "do something." It set up an Office of Youth Camp Safety that required every summer camp to provide the ministry and parents with detailed itineraries of overnight hikes and other hazardous activities. Anxiety was relieved across the land.

The quaint Kingdom of Boravia was booming with tourism. Hotels, conference centers, restaurants, and shopping plazas threatened charming valleys and rugged coasts. The Royal Coastal Commission decided to "do something." It promulgated a regulation requiring an environmental-impact statement for every proposed construction project.

If beauty or ecology were in danger, the report would provide grounds for preventing development. Despair turned to glee. Who could deny that such a scheme would save Boravia's natural charms?

"Doing" the Impossible

A common thread runs through these cases—in each of them someone does something about a problem without solving it. Walking along sidewalks in Regiment City still demands vigilance and nimble feet. The casualty rate at summer camps has not changed measurably. New construction in once scenic Boravia has not been retarded.

These instances of "doing something" belong to the Breakloop Behavior Type known among learned observers as the *Shiftscheme Response.*

In Shiftscheme jobs, functionaries are asked to do what is impossible. They are expected to undertake what no one could accomplish. Their response is to shift attention and energy away from the hopeless task and toward one that can be done and done well. Faced with a problem that is beyond their power to solve, astute administrators resort to "doing something" about it. While the distinction may not be immediately clear, "doing something" about a problem is quite different from actually solving it.

Scarcely any official has the omnipresence to monitor canine bowel movements and juvenile camp wanderings, or to curb land development. However, all administrators have the sense, when all else fails, to issue edicts, establish bureaus, and enact procedures. Memoranda, staff studies, task forces, coordinating committees, programs, and projects are Shiftscheme tools for drawing attention away from futile aims and toward vigorous surrogate efforts.

Shifting a Scheme

It is the dilemma of Shiftschemes that impossible new demands are piled atop a job already so burdensome that attempting Task A is to deny Task B.

The saving grace of the Shiftscheme is the inability of his superiors to measure work performance. Few bosses could recognize genuine accomplishment if it took them to lunch. The wily Shiftscheme undertakes feasible Project X as evidence of trying to solve insolvable Problem Z. Project X will solve nothing; yet bosses, the public, and the press will be none the wiser.

Fueling Around

BREAKLOOP BEHAVIOR REPORT #1

Problem: National shortage of crude oil.

Administrative Insolvability: The shortage was the result of Middle East politics, national policies on fuel pricing, and the indifference of citizens toward saving energy. No authority hierarchy had the power to deal with any of these causes.

Shiftscheme Response: The management of Behemoth Conglomerated Industries cranked up a program of mandatory car pooling for its employees. Ninety percent of the employee parking places were reserved for car-pool vehicles.

Car pooling appeals to common sense as a solution to a fuel shortage. If fewer cars are driven to work, less gasoline will be consumed. Ergo, conservation reduces the shortage.

Herding workers into car pools is, however, difficult for the same reason that mass transit does not work. Everybody lives someplace else. No sooner had Behemoth announced its plan than employees besieged the personnel offices with claims for exemption. Each appeal for exemption had to be reviewed individually. Clerks were added to the personnel staff; then supervisors were added to manage the clerks. Behemoth's public-relations office hired communication specialists to sell car pooling to employees.

Did the car-pooling scheme save the country from an oil crisis? No. Behemoth Conglomerated lacked the power and the charter to do so.

BREAKLOOP BEHAVIOR REPORT #2

Problem: Same crude oil shortage.

Administrative Insolvability: The same lack of power by an organization to deal with the causes of the shortage.

Shiftscheme Response: The United States Auto Club decreed a rule, limiting championship race cars to 114 gallons of fuel for every 200 miles. In race after race, speed ovals were littered with cars that simply ran out of fuel before they could finish.

Did the USAC scheme conserve crude oil? No. Championship race cars burn methanol alcohol, which is distilled from wood, not crude oil.

Overstepping the Bounds

An ingredient common to both these illustrations—and to Shiftscheme situations everywhere—is the impossibility of true solutions. While the causes of the problem at hand are well outside the organizations' formal, legal powers, nonetheless, in case after case, authority hierarchies struggle futilely to control events beyond their limited realm.

Behemoth Conglomerated could not conserve fuel because it could not monitor acceleration habits in thousands of private cars. But since it owned employee parking lots, it did what it could.

The impossibility of controlling private gas pedals is echoed in equally impotent attempts to control light switches, thermostats, doors, windows, and air conditioners.

Modern organizations have formal authority over their members only during work hours. When limited organization authority tries to follow people into their cars, homes, voting booths, or stores, then real solutions will be elusive. A Shiftscheme Response is a common recourse of managers who must demonstrate "constructive action."

Mandatory Voluntarism

BREAKLOOP BEHAVIOR REPORT #3

Problem: Inflation in the Republic of Garfoon reached an annual rate of 4½ percent.

Administrative Insolvability: The problem was neither economic nor bureaucratic. It was political. The power of diverse interest groups in Garfoon prevented Parliament from reducing government spending. That limit on thrift compelled the Bank of Garfoon to jack up the money supply. The mechanics of money systems, arcane and impenetrable, kept the public from guessing that the government itself was behind rising prices. Not surprisingly, the Garfoonians turned to their government to lead the fight against the sinister forces of inflation.

Shiftscheme Response: Enact voluntary wage and price guidelines.

The Shiftscheme Compulsion

Because what Shiftscheme Responses attempt to do is objectively unachievable, administrators eventually must resort to force. While officials are always surprised by the meager participation in voluntary compliance, it is silly to expect people to do voluntarily what they cannot do at all.

Nonetheless, scarcely does a day pass without the launching of another voluntary Shiftscheme crusade. After studying numerous instances of Shiftscheme Response, we have synthesized them into a universal three-step evolution from initial voluntary phase to final mandatory state.

This immutable process, set in motion the moment a program is announced to be "voluntary," is known as the *Shiftscheme Compulsion.*

STEP 1. JAWBONING. A Shiftscheme Response is unveiled to combat a pressing difficulty; everyone is expected to comply willingly. The Prime Minister of Garfoon exhorted Garfoonians to hold the line on wages and prices, as a matter of patriotic duty.

STEP 2. GETTING TOUGH. When Jawboning doesn't work as well as they had expected, Shiftscheme managers "clarify" the ways in which people can comply. A Wage and Price Board was established in Garfoon to monitor Voluntary compliance with the anti-inflation program, write guidelines, and publicize the names of firms that did not meet the standards.

STEP 3. LOWERING THE BOOM. Concluding that few people, even with prodding, will do the right thing on their own, Shiftscheme executives resign themselves to the obvious: mandatory compliance. Step 2 failed in Garfoon; the price index shot to a 12 percent annual rate. As a result, the Wage and Price Board was given stern enforcement powers.

Barking up the Wrong Tree

The irresistible logic of the Shiftscheme Compulsion parallels the seductiveness of the Organizing Trap. If something is good, organize it. If a Shiftscheme program is worth having, it must be required. The urge to coerce abounds. Ritual appeals to duty are invariably followed by controls. It cannot be otherwise.

Shiftscheme Responses, by definition, are aimed at symptoms, not causes. Had voluntary compliance with wage and price guidelines in Garfoon reached 100 percent, inflation would not have abated a jot. Had Garfoonians gleefully refused pay increases, inflation would not have been affected one bit.

Papering Over a Problem

BREAKLOOP BEHAVIOR REPORT #4

Problem: Insure that fire trucks purchased by the Ministry of Forests for fighting forest fires do not break down in the heat of battle.

Administrative Insolvability: Irregular maintenance, driving habits, and vehicle manufacturing defects can conspire to cause mechanical failure. No purchasing official can prevent it. But he can "do something" about it.

Shiftscheme Response: The Ministry of Forests issued detailed specifications, running to 155 pages, for the purchase of fire trucks.

So forbidding were the 155 pages of particulars that only two vendors submitted bids on small fire trucks for rugged terrain. The winning bid was $35,000 per unit. Similarly equipped vehicles were available from manufacturers' catalogues for only $24,000 each.

BREAKLOOP BEHAVIOR REPORT #5

Problem: Protect workers from injury in industrial settings.

Administrative Insolvability: A galaxy of factors—worker habits, supervisory inattention, and misuse of safety equipment, to name a few—can lead to industrial injuries; but none is within the metaphysical power of any agency to monitor or control.

Shiftscheme Response: The Commission on Industrial Safety published an encyclopedia of safety rules and standards that filled a bookshelf six feet long. A third of these regulations were mere homilies (e.g., "Act with care in all situations"). Half of them conflicted with existing public-health laws. And the remainder were unreadable. The industrial accident rate did not diminish.

Promulgate or Perish

Managers cannot resist the compulsion to "do something" even when nothing can be done.

It matters not at all that the safety commission cannot prevent industrial casualties. What is important is that the commission not appear indifferent to the well-being of workers.

Likewise, the Ministry of Forests' Project Manager for Fire Systems Development cannot design an infallible fire truck. But he has to "do something" about the reliability of ministry fire trucks. So he writes 155 pages of specifications.

Papering over a problem—with promulgations, memoranda, regulations, operating procedures, standards, guidelines, and instruction manuals—is a classic Shiftscheme Response to impossible demands. None should be surprised that responsible officials deal with difficulty by throwing paper at it. The wonder is that we expect them to do otherwise.

Throwing Money at the Problem

BREAKLOOP BEHAVIOR REPORT #6

Problem: Decaying neighborhoods in Painted Flats.

Administrative Insolvability: Family disintegration, economic circumstances, rent controls, property-tax inequities, flight of employers to the suburbs, political machinations, and cultural heritage conspire to breed urban decay. Few of the causes are amenable to solution by the Metropolitan Housing Authority. Still, it must do something.

Shiftscheme Response: Throw money at the problem.

The Metropolitan Housing Authority unveiled a grand plan to finance a $200 million Urban Uplift Demonstration Project in Painted Flats. Two square miles of slums were to be demolished to make way for the Compulsion Harbor Center—a complex of stores, hotels, restaurants, offices, theaters, and high-rise middle-income apartments. Millions more were allocated for experimental early childhood education programs, in-home tutoring services, neighborhood medical clinics, and technical training shops.

BREAKLOOP BEHAVIOR REPORT #7

Problem: A 24 percent unemployment rate among rural youth in Triplicate Valley.

Administrative Insolvability: Mechanized farming, rural land prices, and a declining market for the valley's chief crop, parsnips, combined to reduce the number of available jobs for young people. Nothing within the official powers of the national government could treat these problems at their roots.

Shiftscheme Response: Throw money at the problem.

The Ministry of Labor created the Jobs for Youth program with a $950 million budget. This endeavor featured skills assessment, career counseling, and grants to hire chronically unemployed youths.

Spending money is evidence enough that an official is "doing something" about a problem. When the money flows, only an occasional cynic will fail to be convinced that the best of all solutions is being applied.

The Committee Complex

BREAKLOOP BEHAVIOR REPORT #8

Problem: The Endangered Species Act of 1973 prohibited Federal construction projects that threatened plants or animals in danger of extinction. Controversy erupted when the nearly completed Tellico Dam was discovered to be a danger to a three-inch-long fish known as the snail darter. The government was caught between the claims of water management interests and the protests of environmentalists.

Shiftscheme Response: Creation of a seven-member interagency committee to deal with such controversies in the future.

BREAKLOOP BEHAVIOR REPORT #9

Problem: The board of trustees of the Volunteer Coordinating Center ordered its executive director, Doogood, to straighten out the Friend in Need Drive (FIND). Doogood knew that the program's troubles defied simple executive action. Volunteers were difficult to attract and keep. A government subsidy to the Coordinating Center required FIND to accommodate court-referred youths. As a result, the program's capacity to find and screen suitable adults could not keep pace with the influx of teen-agers. Yet unless the program served court-referred youths, the center would lose its subsidy. The causes of the problem, and therefore its real solution, lay beyond Doogood's powers. Nevertheless, Doogood had to do something. Doing nothing, even in the face of the impossible, is morally unacceptable.

Shiftscheme Response: Appoint a committee. Doogood set up a Youth in Crisis Task Force consisting of himself, a center trustee, an adult volunteer, and a local judge. Thereby he turned dilemma to advantage. Even though the task force can't solve the real problem, its very existence will convince the government that something is "being done." The lesson for clever administrators is clear: when maneuvered into a corner, appoint a committee. Any other tactic leaves things to chance.

Bureaucratic Buildup

Everyone imagines that a decisive administrator is non-bureaucratic. Yet, as sophisticated students of organizing well know, decisiveness is a prolific parent of bureaucracy. The Regiment City Public Health Office expanded in order to enforce the pooper-scooper law. The Ministry of Public Concern swelled with inspectors and regional enforcement coordinators to keep an official eye on the safety of summer camps. Processing environmental-impact statements in Boravia employed hundreds of planners and civil engineers. Personnel departments throughout Behemoth Conglomerated hired scores of clerks to handle files and hear appeals about car pooling. Garfoon appointed a host of lawyers, economists, and publicists to administer wage and price controls. And so it goes, wherever the futile Shiftscheme Response is embraced.

Nevertheless, administrators facing impossible tasks must turn to the Shiftscheme Response. All other responses leave them in danger.

Bureaucratic Man

Breakloop managers have no financial "bottom line" to tell them what to do. Fabled Economic Man is guided by an analysis of costs and benefits. Bureaucratic Man, in contrast, can calculate costs; he cannot calculate Breakloop benefits. Therefore, he must concoct surrogate scores. Promulgating elaborate Shiftscheme contrivances in response to demands that he cannot actually fulfill is one way to cope with the Breakloop dilemma of costs without benefits.

Chapter 8

The Firecracker Response

If You Can't Do It Well, Do It Big

Much outcry,
Little outcome.
—Aesop

When the Multiphase Cross Mode Metabolizer was uncrated in the laboratory of Regiment City Medical Center, the board of trustees and chief of staff gathered for photographs. The hospital's press officer boasted that the device made RCMC a leader in advanced medical technology. Three other hospitals in the Regiment Bay area installed metabolizers within a year.

A course in how to cope with the exasperating problems of everyday life was required for seniors in a California high school. The principal explained that the course would give students "the tools necessary to make intelligent decisions in adulthood" and teach them how to make small repairs around the house.

The Commission on Paperwork organized an Office of the Ombudsman to hear complaints about government forms. The ombudsman could be reached on a toll-free number.

These are instances of the Breakloop Behavior Type known as the *Firecracker Response*. A Firecracker can hardly make an error. But Firecrackers can win. Indeed, they must strive to win more accolades, trophies, and press attention than competing Firecrackers.

It is in the nature of the job that Firecrackers cannot do

anything substantial. What they do is little connected to an organization's purposes. No way exists to assess their worth to the system.

Where genuine outputs cannot guide internal decisions to promote people and allocate resources, systems often turn to things that are highly visible, even astonishing.

Prototype of the Species

The prototype of the Firecracker is the politician. The reward or punishment for any particular political decision is either indirect or missing altogether. The greatest rewards accrue to the politician with the greatest flair for catching the public eye. Appearance and symbol prevail over substance.

A Firecracker Taxonomy

From our research, three classes of Firecracker Response have been perceived: BUTTON-DOWN BARNUM, PEACOCK PROFESSIONALIST, and SELF-ADVANCER.

Button-Down Barnum

Publicity stunts and promotional gimmicks are the stock-in-trade of these blatant Firecrackers.

FIRECRACKER ARCHIVE FILE BB-1

System Purpose: Bay Area Rapid Transit exists, in theory, to provide punctual, safe, and economical commuter rail service to San Francisco and Oakland.

Firecracker Response: The director of marketing and communications launched a $113,000 campaign to sell blue canvas tote bags that implored all who saw them to *Go BART*.

FIRECRACKER ARCHIVE FILE BB-2

System Purpose: The municipal government of Cowley Glen

is supposed to make citizens secure in their persons and property, while administering local endeavors that are needed but not otherwise economical.

Firecracker Response: The city manager bought a fleet of minibuses and painted them in psychedelic designs. Despite their token ten-cent fare, the Cowley Glen minibuses rarely had passengers. Indeed, the little buses had nowhere to go. By law they could not leave Cowley Glen, because all inter-city transit was the exclusive province of the Metropolitan Transit Authority. Nonetheless, pictures of the minibuses appeared in magazines and newspapers across the land, her-alding them as a bold innovation.

FIRECRACKER ARCHIVE FILE BB-3

System Purpose: By its own description, the function of the popular television talk show "Here and Now" is to bring enlightenment and controversy to debates on current issues.

Firecracker Response: The producers of "Here and Now" invariably schedule celebrities rather than serious scholars. During the inflation crisis in Garfoon, the only economics expert "Here and Now" booked was L. Forbusch Buckwell, who had recently published a novel.

Peacock Professionalist

The work of Button-Down Barnums is clearly unrelated to the real work of their organizations. Other Firecracker Responses are not so obvious. They have camouflaged their uselessness with the mantle of self-importance, professional-ism, and altruistic service to a larger good. No other Fire-cracker Response is so unrestrained in this public deceit as the Peacock Professionalist.

Peacock Professionalists exploit the mass delusion that "there can't be too much professionalism." They undertake all manner of grand distractions in the name of doing a "good, professional job." Many believe Peacocks act out of public concern. In fact, Peacocks labor to hear the applause of their professional peers. It is the judgment of peers outside their employing organization that concerns Peacocks most. They often regard employing hierarchies as necessary evils that owe them budgets and resources. They unveil innovations and breakthroughs not so much to help their present employer as to impress the next one.

A few examples are sufficient to penetrate their self-righteous plumage.

FIRECRACKER ARCHIVE FILE PP-1

System Purpose: Personnel departments are thought to exist to provide properly screened and trained employees and administer benefit programs.

Firecracker Response: To the accompaniment of press releases, television interviews, professional journal articles, and bulletin-board posters, Flashmore, personnel manager of Melancholy Motors' main assembly plant, instituted the Joy of Work Program. Through films and seminars he imbued plant foremen with the Joy of Work Principle that workers should not be imprisoned by the boredom of doing repetitive tasks. Rather, they should work at a variety of things. Subsequently, one assembly-line worker, caught up in the newfound diversity, neglected to reorder chassis bolts before a part bin ran low. The entire plant shut down for a day while the necessary bolts were acquired.

FIRECRACKER ARCHIVE FILE PP-2

System Purpose: The District Attorney of San Francisco is needed to prosecute criminal cases on the public's behalf.

Firecracker Response: Time magazine reported that an assistant DA, Ray Bonner, created the Complaint Mobile, a baby-blue van that offered free legal services to the poor in their own neighborhoods. The project was celebrated for gaining redress for consumer complaints. In one case, the unit got back a twenty-cent soda-bottle deposit for a small boy. In the first year the Complaint Mobile used a $35,000 federal grant to recover $7,500 for wronged citizens.

FIRECRACKER ARCHIVE FILE PP-3

System Purpose: The Champaign-Urbana Mass Transit District's function is to run clean, safe buses on convenient routes.

Firecracker Response: A new director ordered a fleet of buses in a variety of hues to match color-coded routes. Green buses served the Green Line, lavender buses served the Lavender Line, and so on through a rainbow of colors. While most riders knew immediately where the old University Avenue bus was headed, almost no one could remember where the orange bus would go.

FIRECRACKER ARCHIVE FILE PP-4

System Purpose: Pyramid Point Public Library exists to provide books in a quiet setting.

Firecracker Response: Biblichic, the newly appointed head librarian, renamed the library the Regional Learning Resources Center. He announced that the center would offer classes in kite flying, tell bedtime stories to youngsters, sponsor a model railroad club, and construct practice rooms for aspiring rock musicians. "Being a Learning Resources Center," he explained at his first monthly press conference, "means not having to say you're sorry when people complain that it is too noisy for reading."

Self-Advancer

Unable to relate their work to their organizations' goals, some functionaries are compelled to measure their performance by the progress of their own careers. The Self-Advancer Response is distinguished by the lack of any pretense of serving official ends. What Self-Advancers do, they do for themselves.

FIRECRACKER ARCHIVE FILE SA-1

System Purpose: The charter of the government-funded non-profit Inner City Renaissance Project (ICRP) was to fill the gaps of counsel and assistance for the poor and elderly left by the traditional welfare bureaus.

Firecracker Response: The ICRP set up the two-acre Regiment Farm on vacant lots in the midst of decaying apartment buildings, abandoned factories, and noisy freeways. "Learning about farming is learning about life," exclaimed Brightspark, the executive director of Inner City Renaissance. Urban activists lauded the farm as "innovative" and "ahead of its time." Brightspark was soon appointed a deputy secretary in the Ministry of Public Concern.

FIRECRACKER ARCHIVE FILE SA-2

System Purpose: The *Alumni Bulletin* of Prestigious University is supposed to inform alumni about developments at their alma mater and to keep them up to date on their classmates.

Firecracker Response: When aggressive young Pagesmith was named editor of the *Bulletin,* he converted it from a collection of chatty class notes into a slick, four-color magazine filled with social commentary by renowned scholars and features by expensive freelance writers. In no time, the Prestigious *Bulletin* was sought after by non-alumni to grace coffee tables and doctors' waiting rooms. News of the university and old school ties were relegated to a tear-out supplement distributed only to graduates. The magazine achieved wide distribution and attracted a wealth of advertising revenue. Pagesmith accepted the position of vice-president for advising alumni publications with the National Association of Alma Maters.

FIRECRACKER ARCHIVE FILE SA-3

System Purpose: Trendy Heights High School is supposed to impart learning.

Firecracker Response: The assistant superintendent for instruction, Dr. Glimmer, unveiled the Modular Time Utilization System, in which thirty-minute learning blocks replaced traditional fifty-five-minute classes. Dr. Glimmer explained that "Mod Time" would free students to "pursue individual self-enrichment and interface with teachers in unstructured dyads." Today, Dr. Glimmer is with the Ministry of Education as director of innovative programs.

Gobbling Up Groceries

No one appears less bureaucratic than the showy and often self-righteous Firecrackers. But cut off from a true yardstick of their real worth to a system, they gobble up organization groceries and leave in their wake a bureaucratic residue of offices, programs, and staffs.

Firecrackers rarely contribute to systems, but they can distort and drain them. Usually an organization's top management ignores the predictable pyrotechnics of the Firecracker. At worst, management is grateful for so many "professional" efforts.

Chapter 9

The Blunderfret Adaptation

You Can't Be Too Careful

I love my fellow-creatures—I do all the good I can—
Yet everybody says I'm such a disagreeable man!
—W. S. Gilbert

An inbound overseas airliner with engine trouble was notified that Kennedy Airport in New York was closed because of bad weather. The alternate landing site was Bradley Field at Windsor Locks, Connecticut, where fog was closing in. As the plane circled, the customs official at Bradley refused to allow it to land because he had no inspectors available.

A man in Chicago found a skunk in his garage. Neither the police, the city zoo, the SPCA, federal conservation officials, nor the municipal dogcatcher had jurisdiction over skunks. After the man trapped the skunk, he was cited for trapping without a license and warned that keeping, releasing, or killing the skunk were each against the law.

Before the fall of Saigon in 1975, Flying Tigers Air Freight and Seaboard World Airlines humanely but illegally airlifted hundreds of Vietnamese orphans to the United States. When the planes arrived, a US immigration officer dutifully fined the airlines for each child they had brought into the country.

A Prosperity, South Carolina, high school senior, with excellent grades, missed thirty-five school days while representing her state at a youth leadership conference in Europe and a national 4-H congress in Chicago. Because of her absenteeism, school board officials would not allow her to be graduated with her class.

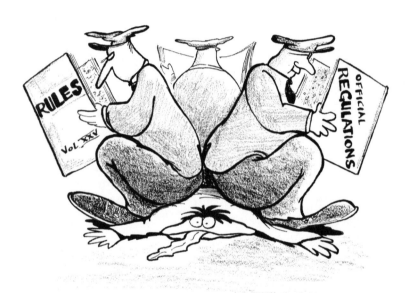

Night nurses at Regiment City Hospital regularly wake sleeping patients at 3 A.M. in order to administer sleeping pills.

The authorities in each of these tales of frustration—the airport customs official, the cops in Chicago, the immigration officer, the South Carolina school trustees, and the nurses—have something in common. Each is forced into the *Blunderfret Adaptation.*

Undefeated—Or Else

A Blunderfret can't win.

He can't impress the boss. He can't get an award for doing an outstanding job.

But he can make a mistake. And one mistake is one too many.

If you can't win but can only lose, you will be obsessed with the possibility of blunders. In a job where one mistake can end a career, obsessive caution is the only reasonable behavior.

A classic Blunderfret job is the disbursing officer. Disbursements are either right or wrong. One correct disbursement is no better than any other. There is no prize for Disbursement of the Year, no silver cup for the most professional processing of a travel voucher.

If a disbursing officer's job denies him even the possibility of winning a gold star, what does he do? He worries a lot about making the single mistake—letting a fraud or embezzlement slip past—that can ruin him forever. He doesn't think about winning at all, only about how to prevent losing.

Tiptoeing through a Minefield

People in Blunderfret jobs everywhere work assiduously to protect themselves from error. They are cautious, security-minded, self-protective. They can't be risk takers. Indeed, Blunderfrets embody what we mean by "bureaucrat." They worship rules, go by the book, cherish written procedures, devise forms, and pick nits.

A Blunderfret copes with his fear of a fatal error by embracing caution and red tape. Contrast his work with a high-risk Demand Loop job such as a commodity market speculator. A speculator can, in a single day, either ruin himself financially or get rich. He can lose big, but, unlike a Blunderfret, he can also win big. Pressure comes from taking risks. Blunderfrets are never tempted to take risks; they can't win if they do. The only risk left is the chance of an error. If a Blunderfret goes by the book, follows rules to the letter, and double-checks all the forms, no one can blame *him* if something goes wrong. Thereby does he ease the anxiety of error.

Passing the Buck

In the land of the Blunderfrets, the rule book is holy writ. But not even the thickest rule book can cover everything. Inevitably there will arise a baffling case that will not fit into any of the accepted categories no matter how hard a Blunderfret squeezes and pushes. In such cases he takes all of the relevant documents to his boss for a decision. He shifts responsibility to someone else, kicks the problem upstairs, passes the buck.

The Blunderfret dares not make a decision on a case not covered by the rules. Going beyond the rules means taking a chance. Not taking chances is the only thing he can do.

Missing the Roots

The trouble we have with Blunderfrets is that we keep expecting them to do what they can't. We blame the postal clerk for long lines and forget that the fault lies in the design of the postal system. We focus on personalities; we should be looking at how Breakloop systems dispense carrots and wield sticks.

Suffering a grumpy railroad conductor, we are unfair in asking, "What's the matter with *him?*" *He* isn't the problem; the nature of his job is the problem. A cross and unyielding railroad conductor has learned—and been reminded for years—that he can't win by taking chances or bending the rules. He has learned that to be cranky is to survive. Sweetness he saves for his grandchildren. His sole reward is seniority, his only goal daily survival. He must keep from getting caught by train inspectors or ticket auditors. No free riders on his train. No dirty boots on the mohair either.

Blunderfrets Observed

Officials at the Department of Health, Education and Welfare threaten to cut off financial aid if school boards fail to file affirmative action compliance questionnaires on time —even if the school district receives no HEW money.

A US postal inspector crushed the competitive mail-delivery business of a teenager in South Carolina by warning his mother.

During a prolonged drought the Greater London Council announced that its river engineers would begin their annual flood alert on the Thames.

An Alabama building inspector ordered the demolition of a children's tree house that was not set back twenty feet from a city street.

The New York City Tax Department regularly mails annual bills for property tax to the owner of every building. When the New York University Medical Center failed to pay for a number of years in a row, the tax collector automatically started a repossession action in court even though universities and hospitals are exempt from property taxes.

Railroad tank cars loaded with chlorine were sidetracked for defective wheel bearings forty miles from their destination, a municipal sewage treatment plant. Because they were carrying hazardous cargo, they were not permitted to complete their journey. Instead, the railroad ordered the cars hauled to a repair shop one hundred miles in the opposite direction.

You can't be too careful.

The Job Made Me Do It

Crunchcrumb has savings and checking accounts at the Bank of Regiment Bay. His home mortgage is also with the bank, and he carries its credit card. Nonetheless, when Crunchcrumb presents a check drawn on the BRB for cash, the teller examines it as if it were a three-dollar bill, demands three pieces of personal identification from Crunchcrumb, and retires to a back room for a superior's approval. Crunchcrumb waits an average of twenty minutes on line and thirteen more at the teller's window each time he tries to cash a check.

Dealing with Blunderfrets is exasperating, but the point is that they cannot act any other way. Caution must prevail in handling money.

Trust Not

As banks cannot leave questionable transactions to tellers' judgments, gambling casinos dare not leave the management of gaming tables to trust alone. Blackjack dealers in a Harrah's casino must comply with rule books running to over two hundred pages. Some casinos have fifty such manuals prescribing everything from window washing to public decorum. Card dealers must shuffle decks, collect bets, and handle cash with precise hand movements. Any deviation from the stipulated practice draws supervisory attention to the possibility that an employee is palming the casino's revenue.

Assuredly, such procedures may be exasperating to dealer and player alike. The casino, however, has no choice but to design a system that minimizes trust while maximizing predictability. The security of $500 million in small bills passing through the hands of employees every year cannot be left to honesty.

In the gaming business nothing is left to chance.

Better Safe than Sorry

Babysitters in Illinois who care for children more than ten hours a week must meet state standards for licensing. Fines or jail sentences are prescribed for those who fail to comply. Where children are concerned, what conscientious functionary can leave things to happenstance?

In Iowa an imaginative school superintendent put cartoon characters on the sides of school buses so that children too young to read could find their homeward-bound bus. State safety inspectors condemned this as a deviation from federal guidelines requiring that school buses be all yellow. No one in the transportation hierarchy can say why cartoon decals on a school bus are a safety hazard. But if the rules do not allow them, no safety inspector will risk the heat of federal review just so children can get home from school.

You Can't Be Too Careful

The system by which the Food and Drug Administration approves or rejects new drugs is an example of Blunderfret behavior. Since the thalidomide horror in 1962, FDA has had veto power over the introduction of new drugs into US medical practice.

The FDA has no systematic incentive to expedite the release of new drugs, not even for the cure of cancer. What thanks would it get? The glory would go to the company that developed the drug. So would the profits. The scientists who did the basic research might become Nobel laureates. (Jonas Salk's polio vaccine made his name a household word.) But what reward would there be for the FDA if it hurried a miracle drug's release? No cover of *Time* for the director. No television talk-show interviews for the enforcement officials. No promotion. No pay raise. Not even an honorable mention.

All the FDA can consider is the potential risk of the drug's doing harm. Suppose side effects appeared? Suppose some patients became disfigured—or died? The entire project would be a national scandal. And who would be blamed? The scientists? Unlikely. They worked to rid mankind of a dread affliction. The drug company? A little, perhaps, but it did everything required under the FDA's procedures for testing new drugs. No, the villain would be the FDA. Editorials would demand drug-testing procedures that are more thorough. Congress would begin hearings into drug-approval safeguards. Careers would be ruined. The FDA would have made the error that is one too many in the Blunderfret world.

The Fault Is Not Theirs

Every bureaucrat with veto power worries that this might happen to him. It must be in the back of his mind every time he faces an official yes or no decision. That is why procedural foot-dragging is endemic to regulatory bureaus. They must always require more tests. The more tests, the greater the proof that an agency tried to do all it could to protect the public.

The visible effect of FDA's caution is that the nation is saved from a possible medical catastrophe.

The invisible effect is that some people may die of cancer unnecessarily. But no one can measure the unseen good an unavailable drug might have done. No one can weigh its unknown benefits against official calculation of its possible harm. In the Blunderfret world there is never an opportunity to weigh the good against the bad. Since we will hear only of the possible bad effects we were spared, we will surely not guess that we have lost anything at all because of regulatory timidity.

The lesson is that we can't blame individual Blunderfrets for their authoritarian, officious behavior. That's looking in the wrong place. We must look instead at the structure of their jobs. Only then can we learn why obstructive functionaries behave the way they do. Only then can we learn that the Blunderfret has no opportunity to win, that he can't win gold stars no matter what he does, that he is driven to shield himself from black marks. No wonder, then, that they fret over the possibility of blunders.

Chapter 10

The Turnstile Adaptation

Sober Dedication to the Wrong Thing

*The task he undertakes
Is numb'ring sands . . .*
—Richard II

The national image of the Boy Scouts of America was compromised when scoutmasters in thirteen cities were caught padding membership lists with fictitious names.

A former employee of American Airlines reports that the job performance of cabin attendants was evaluated on the number of "friendly facial expressions" and "eye-to-eye contacts" made with passengers.

Soviet factories have quotas for making automobiles. The system gives rewards for the number of finished automobiles delivered out the factory door. However, there are no rewards for making spare parts. Therefore, few spare parts are produced.

These instances of maximizing numerical scoreboards are a Breakloop Behavior Type known far and wide as the *Turnstile Adaptation*.

Confusing Inputs and Outputs

Turnstiles share a common reaction to dread uncertainty. All of them adapt to Breakloop feedback deprivation by counting things. Mostly they count system inputs. Certainly they are not counting outputs. They think they are. But they can't. Breakloop systems have *no* measurable outputs. In the

Breakloop world, inputs are universally confused with outputs.

Inputs are the only thing Turnstiles can count.

Few Boy Scout leaders can resist the commonsense temptation to regard the number of boys in their program as its output. It is an unavoidable confusion. The more boys in the program, the more organizational merit badges the leaders themselves get.

An airline's purpose is swift, efficient transportation. It is, however, difficult, even in a Demand Loop, to relate the performance of cabin attendants to an airline's goals. No wonder, then, that American fixes on the frequency of smiles and eye contacts as a measure of a cabin attendant's performance.

No Win, No Lose

The Turnstile is the most common and the most comfortable of the Breakloop Behavior Types. In pure form, Turnstiles rarely can either win or lose. They are immune to job pressure.

The only way harm can befall a Turnstile is if he personally cheats the system. Consider the case of Tallymark, regional distribution manager for Snapback Girdle and Truss Company. Tallymark's job is to move goods out of a regional warehouse. The best tool Snapback has to assess his managerial performance is the minimization of inventory levels. It is not surprising that Tallymark fraudulently ships more goods than Snapback's customers have actually ordered. The customers, of course, return the excess. Moreover, Snapback must pay the shipping costs both ways. In the short run Tallymark looks good.

Tallymark will go on falsifying shipments until Snapback's auditor wants to know why shipping costs are so high. Then his mistaken zeal, like that of the enrollment-padding Boy Scout leaders, will do him in.

Distorting the Function

Personal cheating engendered by the Turnstile obsession with simple quantification is, happily, rare. More frequent and more damaging are the cases where Turnstile adaptations legally distort and shift the whole work pattern of an organization. This occurs in two ways.

The Easy-Collar Model

An Arresting Temptation

Under J. Edgar Hoover, the Federal Bureau of Investigation pursued automobile thieves rather than battle drug abuse and organized crime. Car thieves are, in the argot of law enforcement, "easy collars." Nabbing them was an easy way to boost the monthly performance figures.

The FBI worried more about its total case load than about putting away Mafia chieftains. Showing that 91 percent of all investigations led to arrests was the road to public support and fatter budgets.

A Simple Deduction

The Revenue Service chases delinquent blue-collar taxpayers rather than those who are business or professional people. The service, having no way to judge its public benefit, must weigh the number of delinquent tax cases it closes as performance. There is no Turnstile advantage in pursuing businessmen, shielded by their accountants and attorneys. It is far more rewarding—to the revenue agent and the system—to attach the salary of a helpless wage earner.

Revenue auditors operate on much the same principle. Middle-income tax returns can be reviewed quickly. What auditor will then bother with the complexities of a million-aire's tax return when performance is measured by the number of cases he closes?

Cops and Harlots

Policemen are often subject to formal reviews of their job performance. Performance may be measured by the number of arrests. Obviously, some arrests are easier to make than others.

Street muggers and burglars abound. But paddy wagons haul in hookers on a regular schedule.

Prostitutes are highly visible. They are easy to collar. They are distasteful to decent citizens. And they rarely carry guns.

Few can resist the commonsense temptation to think of the number of arrests as the output of a police department. Fewer still can grasp the reality that arrests are inputs to the criminal justice system.

Easier Collars Yet

No social-work agency can measure accomplishment of an intangible goal such as enhancing the lives of its clients. But a welfare agency knows exactly how many cases it handles. Tallying the case load soon becomes the agency's yardstick of the good it is doing. *What* it does for its clients is forever lost in a convenient numbers game.

The social worker must defend the notion that case load is an indicator of performance. He must scoff at the truth that the case load is actually input.

The Privateer Model

All Turnstiles earn organization groceries by counting things. To keep a well-stocked pantry, Turnstiles learn to maximize the count of what their systems reward. The Easy Collar Model of system distortion takes the path of least resistance. Another Turnstile Adaptation is the Privateer Model, in which well-intentioned Turnstiles cheat the outside world on behalf of the organization. Privateers work in systems whose outputs nearly approximate the real functions of Demand Loops. To maximize their count of pseudo-outputs, Privateers engage in deception and fraud.

Not only do systems get distorted in the Privateer process, people often get hurt.

Back in the USSR

Ruins of collapsed buildings litter the Soviet landscape. They are the result of rewarding construction organizations for the *number* of buildings erected. Where quality is not part of their criteria of performance, no one should be surprised that construction crews do not sink piles deep enough to support buildings.

In Siberia, apartments stand vacant and uninhabitable because they were built with plans intended for southern Russia. The rush to get completed buildings into a year's construction quota led to desperate shortcuts in roofing and plumbing.

Pravda discerned the Turnstile Adaptation in a public complaint that the only sound construction in the Soviet Union was the wall the Building Materials Ministry has built around itself.

Counting Kids

There are 350,000 children in foster homes in the United States. Most are not available for adoption. Not even their foster parents can adopt them. As long as a child remains in a foster home, he or she remains under the jurisdiction of a child welfare agency. Such agencies are funded according to the *number* of children on their rolls. Every child adopted into a permanent home reduces the agency's funding.

Such a Turnstile system compels social workers to encourage unwed mothers to place their children in foster care. As a consequence of this system distortion, an adoption black market has sprung up. Social workers continue to tell unwed mothers that it will be easier to get their children back from a foster home than from adoptive parents. They don't mention that the funds that pay their salaries depend on how many children they can push into foster homes.

Quantification Prevails

Managers in Breakloop systems make decisions that they must be able to defend against any future charges of being whimsical. The best defense against such challenges is to base a crucial decision on a *number*. Things that are calculable are readily defensible. Consequently, the quantifiable displaces the merely impressionistic. Statistics win every time.

People in an organization soon discover that rewards are distributed according to performance statistics rather than actual performance. Therefore, they labor mightily to achieve the highest count they can. In universities, maximizing the number of research publications—easily countable —long ago pushed aside classroom teaching with its immeasurable outcomes.

Protection by the Numbers

The mission of the Environmental Protection Agency (EPA) is to protect the ecological balance of nature from the ravages of civilization—a Breakloop chore of the highest order. Not surprisingly, the EPA quickly resorted to a Turnstile Adaptation, measuring the *percentage* of hydrocarbons in the air.

Having found excessive hydrocarbon content in the air near a proposed oil shale project, EPA halted it. The poor quality of air near the project, as it turned out, was the result of hydrocarbon emissions from sagebrush.

The stop-construction edict had to be founded on a *number*—however removed that number might be from furthering the intention to protect air from industrial pollution.

The Puff Count

Public-relations specialists count column inches of newspaper stories, client mentions in gossip columns, press releases issued, annual reports written, inquiries answered, tours conducted, awards from PR associations won, and client appearances on talk shows scheduled. It doesn't matter that thirty minutes on an afternoon FM radio talk show won't sell even one $50,000 specialized industrial computer. It's still thirty minutes of air time to be counted.

Many public information officers will insist that counting press releases mailed is a proper measure of their output. They will be puzzled by the uncommon sense that press releases are only inputs.

Attendance Is Paid

Public school superintendents loathe dropouts because their budgets often flow from government subsidies based on enrollment figures. This partly explains the official obsession with attendance, truancy, and student health.

Schools exist to have some effect on students' minds. But the quality of that effect is not accessible to convenient measurement. The Turnstile alternative for evaluating the performance of schools is to calculate enrollments.

Understanding the Turnstile Adaptation to the blind world of Breakloop decision-making requires counter-intuitive thinking. The insight that press releases, school enrollments, arrests of criminals, or welfare case loads are *not* organization outputs flies in the face of common sense. Turnstiles have merchandised inputs as their outputs for so long that only exceptional minds can see that the truth is otherwise.

Chapter 11

The End-Means Inversion

Why Organizations Can't Do What They're Supposed To

It is the tendency of formalism . . .
to substitute means in the room of ends.
— Bishop Pearson

New York City policemen, on duty sixteen consecutive hours trying to flush murderers out of a storefront, were prohibited from eating sandwiches offered by the Salvation Army. Accepting gifts and free food is, according to department rules, "a corruption hazard."

John Zech stopped his car along the shoulder of a Minnesota highway to help a stranded motorist. His reward was a traffic ticket. The highway is posted with signs that warn, "No Stopping Except in Emergency." The emergency was not his.

The United States Employment Service (USES) gets its organizational groceries as long as it has available people for whom it can find jobs. The people for whom it is easiest to find jobs, not surprisingly, are those who already have them. Thus, USES launched a media campaign to encourage professionals to quit their jobs and seek new ones through USES.

The *means* of doing a job triumph over the *goals*. The essence of this curious phenomenon is formulated in the

End-Means Inversion:

The Means Employed to Reach Goals Eventually Come to Replace Those Goals

Output versus Upkeep

Confirmation is all around. US welfare agencies spend billions of dollars each year. Direct distribution of this money to welfare recipients would virtually eliminate poverty. But these billions do not go to the poor. Instead, they go to an army of caseworkers, counselors, planners, urban renewers, development economists, administrative assistants, and assistant administrators. Middle-class professionalism (the means) has engulfed income distribution (the goal).

Television audience ratings, developed originally to measure the popularity of entertainment programs, came to be used as a yardstick of TV news quality as well. To drive up the ratings of news programs, broadcasters have resorted to on-camera slapstick and weather clowns. Viewer ratings (the means) have replaced presenting the news (the goal).

The Comprehensive Employment Training Act was passed as a cure for hard-core unemployment. Instead, local political leaders used the money to hire lawyers, systems analysts, and registered nurses. Hiring people (the means) has supplanted the eradication of unemployment (the goal).

PERT is supposedly a scientific device to monitor organization performance and control its costs. A number of defense contractors have established special departments to prepare detailed monthly PERT reports. The Air Force dutifully files these PERT reports, but no one reads them. Expensive statistical reports (the means) have overrun cost control (the goal).

The Inversion Closer to Home

We should not imagine that the Inversion afflicts only large organizations. It corrupts even the smallest groups.

A recent issue of the Regiment Park Tennis Club newsletter carried an appeal for volunteer typists to rescue the club's officers from a logjam of correspondence, meeting minutes, and committee reports. The lead story in the same issue announced a program to double the club's rolls by encouraging each member to bring in one recruit. The courts were already overbooked, but there was a serious need for new members to serve on committees, work at tournaments, and volunteer for typing. The paperwork *means* had defeated the recreational *end*.

A cooperative day-care center in Triplicate Valley became large enough to require a full-time director. The co-op found just the person it wanted, an energetic young woman with a graduate degree in early childhood development. The center needed a government subsidy to pay the new director's salary. Government subsidies require each parent participating in the center to attend a weekly lecture on "parenting." Soon enough the seminars had heard every child psychologist in Triplicate Valley. Then the director scheduled a lecturer on consumer fraud in the automobile-repair business. Another addressed the evils of pesticides. A third was to show 35-mm slides of the Mayans in Yucatán. The subsidy and its dictates, the *means*, had overcome day care, the *goal*.

In Pyramid Point there was a thriving Chamber Music Society. Nothing elaborate. Just a small group dedicated to bringing concerts to local Bach fans. Within four years the energies of the society's members were dissipated in telephone marathons to raise money. The fund-raising *means* had triumphed over the *goal*, concerts.

How It Happens

We observe that in every case means overcome ends. It is ever so.

Blunderfret Adaptations reduce fear.

Turnstile Adaptations focus busily on the wrong thing. Rules, procedures, and forms shield the Blunderfret from fear and aid the Turnstile in counting. No wonder, then, that these functionaries revere the *ways* they work, quite apart from *what* their work is supposed to accomplish. Consequently, people imbue rules with emotional content far beyond what is needed to get their work done.* When they reach that point, they have gone too far. Blunderfrets make forms sacred and Turnstiles turn statistics into purposes.

Trickle-Down Distortion

Where organization meets problem or system encounters crisis, there is response.

The Firecracker Response hucksters symbol without substance, throwing out sparks in every direction, putting an organization in the position of having to "do something" about a problem or crisis.

The flailing of the Firecracker becomes the impossible demand upon the Shiftscheme. The Shiftscheme Response, in turn, is to organize threats from outside or demands from above into projects, programs, procedures, or committees.

Shiftscheme promulgations set up the work of Blunderfrets and Turnstiles. These latter functionaries finally invert means into ends, casting procedures in bronze and maximizing irrelevant activities while original purposes are lost.

The Brown-Bag Blues

A doubt about whether every child in America was eating a nutritional lunch quickly became a Shiftscheme program

---

* The deforming effect of bureaucratic structure upon personalities has been revealed by Robert K. Merton in *Social Theory and Social Structure, Revised.* New York: the Free Press, 1957.

of Federally funded school lunches. The *purpose* was nutrition; the *means* was tasteless, institutional fare dished up by ladies with nets over their hair. The result: students passed by the subsidized chipped beef on toast to reach junk-food vending machines. The system started out to do one thing and ended up doing another.

Witnessing this daily stampede to the soft-drink and candy machines led some school districts to forsake dietitians and hairnetted ladies to bring in fast-food vendors. The official nutrition goal was inverted again when the fiscal means of counting heads in the cafeteria was served by the enticement of Jumbo Burgers.

No one puts forth the alternative of the brown bag. No one would dare. Leaving lunches to parents is leaving things to chance. Better chipped beef on toast, Baby Ruths, or Big Macs than the uncertainty of a brown bag.

With Charity from All

Once upon a time the assorted charities, youth groups, and other worthy endeavors in Regiment City conducted separate annual fund-raising drives. The collective logic of a single, unified campaign was, however, irresistible.

Thus, Metropolitan Unified Giving (MUG) came to be. Every worker, manager, shopkeeper, schoolchild, and housewife in the city was to be touched for a "fair share" donation.

Unsatisfied with merely *exhorting* everyone in the area, MUG wanted 100 percent *participation*. To promote the spirit of giving, MUG set up public scoreboards listing the percentage of participation for every company, union local, professional organization, merchants association, school, and city block.

In the heat of competition, each group insisted that every last one of its members participate. Competition between business rivals was fierce. Neighboring grade schools took to the challenge with the old school spirit. Adjoining blocks fought to uphold the honor of their turfs.

Reluctant workers were pressured by both foremen and shop stewards. Recalcitrant middle managers were called into meetings with divisional vice-presidents. Miserly mothers found themselves ostracized in neighborhood playgrounds. Fourth-graders who withheld their pennies were left out of schoolyard games.

In MUG's desperate rush to score 100 percent participation, the spirit of charity was trampled. The organization grew. Costs shot up, cutting heavily into the funds available for charitable distribution. With resources committed to securing pledges, collections were neglected. The *means*, keeping score, had conquered the *end*, helping people.

No Free Riders

In our research we have detected a form of End-Means Inversion peculiar to Breakloop organizations which are voluntary in nature. The burden of running a volunteer organization invariably falls on a few dedicated members, while the rest ride along for either the prestige or the fun.

The Adoption Assistance Association (AAA) has a national board with sixty-three members, fifty-one of whom rarely attended the quarterly board meetings or participated in committee work. The national chairwoman, Mrs. Munificence Wellment, tolerated the shirkers for the first half of her term. Then she cracked down. In a letter to the board she called for larger standing committees, the appointment of regional whips to enforce attendance at board meetings, and a requirement that each board member make at least two inspection visits each year to local adoption agencies.

Mrs. Wellment's tough-minded promulgations illustrate

the heretofore unexamined *Free Rider Factor:*

Injustices in Carrying the Burden of Volunteer Work Will Be Remedied by More Organizing.

The Net Result

Every volunteer organization is susceptible to the Free Rider Factor.

We can discern its presence in an organization as casual as the Regiment Park Tennis Club. Club president Netrusher resented those members whose only interest was in playing tennis. Officers of an organization cannot tolerate members who don't at least feign interest in the treasurer's monthly recitation at a four-hour business meeting.

Netrusher reserved particular venom for Fouline. Fouline loved to lob and backhand his way through sunny afternoons but never attended a single meeting and paid his dues only after a third dunning notice.

To assure that everyone in the club did his fair share, Netrusher pushed a new package of rules through the executive committee. As a result, the Regiment Park Tennis Club now has a rotating clean-up duty roster, compulsory attendance at business meetings, mandatory purchase of tickets to the annual Tennis Ball, and a one-year apprenticeship on the Tournament Arrangements Committee before a member can use the club's courts.

Participation in club administration, the *means*, pushed aside the enjoyment of tennis, the *end*. The Free Rider Factor propels maintenance to prevail over purpose.

Build We Must

The Port Authority of New York and New Jersey provides interstate transportation facilities in the New York area.

To accomplish its goals the Authority needs money. Therefore, the Authority built money makers such as bridges, tunnels, airports, container ports, and the World Trade Center. The one thing it didn't build was a mass transit system. Subways and commuter lines simply could not supply enough tolls and fares.

While New York City needed mass transportation, it got crowded highways, airport delays, and air pollution. Efficient transportation, the *end,* was run down by Turnstile coin counting, the *means.*

Turkey Trot

Behemoth Conglomerated Industries hired Bidwell, with his newly minted MBA degree, to fill the post of corporate director of mergers and acquisitions. Never having run a company did not inhibit young Bidwell from buying subsidiaries for Behemoth. He set a personal goal of announcing an acquisition every two months. Since the national antitrust laws prevented Behemoth from merging with firms in its own industry, Bidwell could only buy organizations that no one in the corporation could understand or evaluate. In his zeal to surpass his self-imposed work quota, Bidwell unavoidably acquired a growing flock of business turkeys. As a result, Behemoth ran into unexpected financial losses. The compulsion to acquire firms, a *means,* had rolled over corporate profits, the *goal.*

The Acquisitive Warrior

The Royal Boravian Air Force was lost without battles to fight. Victorious in the last border skirmish, the Air Force suffered a crimp in its feedback loop when the armistice was signed.

In combat, winning or losing was the scoreboard. In peace,

the Air Force invented a surrogate measure of its scoreboard, the number of advanced weapons development projects it undertook.

The peacetime acquisitions of weaponry, a *means*, replaced air superiority, the wartime *objective*.

As a matter of course, Blunderfret and Turnstile Adaptations evolve into End-Means Inversion by raising practice above purpose. In this way do organizations go too far down the road to Diminishing Returns.

It cannot be any other way. The people who pursue silliness or implement the absurd cannot be blamed.

Not to push Blunderfret protectionism and Turnstile maximization to distortion of a system is to leave things to chance.

Nothing will be left to chance.

Chapter 12

The Priority Split

How the Important Work Gets Moved to the Back Burner

We have left undone those things which we ought to have done; and we have done those things which we ought not to have done.

—The Book of Common Prayer

Just about everyone who isn't laboring on an assembly line has two distinct kinds of tasks to perform. First are the jobs that have deadlines or that take place according to a regular schedule. These are *Now* jobs. They include reports, tax audits, whatever the boss is screaming about this morning, and all our daily rituals. The compelling thing about delivering a lecture, compiling a quarterly report, or sharpening pencils is that they are well ordered and familiar tasks.

The second kind of task—the *Later* job—is altogether different. Later jobs include all those good things we *ought* to do even though they lack deadlines or schedules. They can be postponed.

Keeping up with the latest research in your field is a Later task; it's important but you don't have to do it right this minute. The same is true of enhancing your leadership skills, thinking about long-range planning, and grooming your subordinates for advancement. They are all things you

should do. But they are also things you can put off with impunity until tomorrow. And you always do.*

The Priority Split

The crucial difference between Now and Later tasks is that Now work always gets done first. Or else. Now tasks always go to the top of a daily work agenda. There are no exceptions. There can't be.

Try to tell your boss you couldn't get to the weekly production report because you were evaluating the long-range effects that fourth-generation computers will have on staff requirements in fiscal year 2001. Only the financially independent will be tempted.

Later jobs can always go to the bottom of the pile. And do.

The scientific statement of this universal phenomenon is the *Priority Split:*

Scheduled Work Invariably Replaces Unscheduled Work.

Tomorrow Never Comes

Organization theorists James March and Herbert Simon were the first to observe that programmed tasks relentlessly drive unprogrammed jobs out of each workday.

But not only does the Now work get done first, it soon enough becomes virtually the only work that gets done at all. The ultimate difficulty with splitting priorities is that scheduled work soon displaces open-ended tasks. Anything that isn't screaming to get done by yesterday gets put off. And off.

---

* What's true of work is also true of life in general. There are Now jobs and Later jobs in our domestic lives as well as at the office. Paying the mortgage, seeing the dentist about a toothache, and putting out the garbage are Now tasks. Learning Italian, painting the summer cottage, and beginning a rigorous program of exercise can always begin Later.

The result is that many vital things simply don't get done at all.

The Priority Split Observed

Corporate personnel departments originated to train employees and advise management on labor relations policy. These functions demand contemplation, a Later activity. Instead, most modern personnel staffs spend their time on Now tasks such as negotiating labor contracts and managing the company cafeteria.

A university administrator who has two titles will inevitably concentrate on the Now jobs that fall to him as Dean of Behavioral Sciences and postpone the Later responsibilities that are his as Dean of Academic Planning. The demanding nature of departmental problems will eat up his time until none is left for planning.

Why NOW?

Deadlines for Now work have two sources, the boss and oneself.

If the boss said he wants it on his desk by 11 A.M., there is little choice but to comply. Bosses tend to impose structure and deadlines wherever they can.

But a boss can't supervise everything. Even a meticulous superior leaves room for subordinates to arrange their own work priorities.

Thus a lot of priorities get split because *we* crave order. Open-ended assignments confront us with more discomfort than most can bear. We will inevitably create our own deadlines and bring our own structure to the loosest, most freewheeling jobs. Only by forcing ambiguity into crisply routine Now jobs can we overcome dread uncertainty. To quash anxiety, we tend always to fill every vacuum of structure with rules, reports, procedures, and standards of our own devising. It's the only way to "get things done."

The More the Merrier

A Priority Split recently occurred in the Trendy Heights school system. A candidate for the school board found that guidance counselors were burdened with paperwork and problem students. This left little time for career counseling.

The counselors had, not surprisingly, come to concentrate their efforts on daily attendance reports and other paperwork that were the Now tasks built into their jobs. Unruly students consumed what little unprogrammed time remained. No time remained for counseling. The candidate who brought attention to the problem rode it to electoral victory.

As a result the high school principal was allocated budget lines for three more counselors, who were assigned exclusively to counseling, free from the burden of daily paperwork. This was a recipe for dissension among the incumbent counselors. They were doing the dull dirty work while the new counselors drew the "professional" work.

The principal came up with a plan to quell the unrest: divide both the dirty work and the career advising among all the counselors.

Who could oppose such a reasonable solution?

Within months, however, the Priority Split worked its will. The time spent on career counseling was again squeezed out of each day's agenda by the burdens of truancy and the crises of discipline. By the end of the first semester not one of the counselors, old or new, had time to read college bulletins or follow scholarship offerings.

Another Day at the Office

Taskwright, manager of the Random Systems Division of Behemoth Conglomerated Industries, begins his day at 8:30

A.M., when he hangs up his coat, checks to see whether his name is still on the door, gets a Danish and coffee from the coffee wagon, and picks up his morning mail.

Among professional journals and office communiqués is a memo reminding Taskwright of a monthly expense report due Friday and an urgent R & D request for data on structured random systems.

He marks both of these demands on his desk calendar. Today's calendar page reminds him that a quantitative breakdown of ordinal randomness is due to corporate headquarters in the afternoon.

He gets right on it.

At 10:30 A.M., while Taskwright is deep in calculation, a phone call reminds him that he is a member of the luncheon panel at today's meeting of the Regiment regional chapter of the Random Systems Society.

He takes an hour to scan the technical papers that will be read at the meeting. After jotting down a few apt phrases, judiciously balancing constructive criticism with accolades, he dashes to the luncheon.

Back at his desk by 1:30 P.M., Taskwright completes the ordinal randomness report and gets it in the mail by 3:45 P.M.

An hour and fifteen minutes left until quitting time. Taskwright can put off until tomorrow working on the expense report and the data on structured random systems. After all, he has managed to finish one important report and still make it to a professional luncheon. Giving himself a figurative pat on the back, Taskwright goes down the hall to the vending machine for a well-deserved cup of coffee.

Taskwright has a stack of Later jobs sitting on the proverbial back burner. He should keep up with the journal articles in the hotly competitive field of random systems. He ought to write up his own findings on the anomalies of random biases.

He also needs to meet with each of his four randomization analysts to map out their career development programs.

He has promised to outline a course on clear writing for the Division's junior analysts.

He hasn't opened the programmed self-study text on managerial accounting gathering dust on top of his filing cabinet.

Taskwright means to get around to all these things—someday.

But not now.

He is wrung out. Coffee in hand, he wanders to the office of his colleague and friend, Ditherton.

Ditherton is also unwinding after a struggle to meet three report deadlines. He, too, is haunted by a batch of Later projects, but he can scarcely ignore old buddy Taskwright.

By 4:30 P.M. Taskwright walks back to his office. No point in starting anything new at this late hour. Might as well leave early and beat the afternoon commuter rush.

The Now work got done; the Later work didn't. So it goes in offices, shops, and homes across the land.

Chapter 13

The Spin-Off Effect

How the Later Tasks Almost Get Done

*Fanaticism consists in redoubling your
efforts when you have forgotten your aim.*
—George Santayana

To say that Later tasks have no deadlines is not to say they
have no importance. On the contrary, they are vital. Because
Taskwright doesn't keep up with the technology in his field,
Behemoth Conglomerated will get thrashed by competitors
who do. Because Taskwright doesn't get around to mastering
the mysteries of managerial accounting, he will never ascend
to the mahogany suite. Because Taskwright can't find time
to help his assistants develop their management skills, they
will either be wasted as resources or quit, and either way
Behemoth Conglomerated will eventually face a lack of
middle-management talent.

Putting First Things Last

Although Later jobs *are* important, few have time to start
them, and fewer still ever get them done. The importance
of Later jobs remains hidden among the clamor of Now
demands until someone upstairs notices that the organization
is suffering.

It won't happen today. Or even tomorrow. But soon
enough an executive will want to know why Behemoth Conglomerated has fallen behind in, say, the development of
ordinal randomness systems.

Taskwright's defense, that he has been too busy, is air-

tight. Management must finally accept his defense. Task-wright can document how busy he has been—with the Now work—and how little time he has had for the slippery, elusive Later things.

Behemoth management readily appreciates that Task-wright—like busy managers everywhere—is not wholly to blame when Later tasks go undone. Nevertheless, the company must assure that matters vital to its survival are somehow accomplished. Vital tasks cannot be exposed to the uncertainty of perpetual postponement.

The only solution possible is to create a new unit to handle the development of ordinal randomness, the Special Projects Branch. The sole task of this new box on Behemoth's

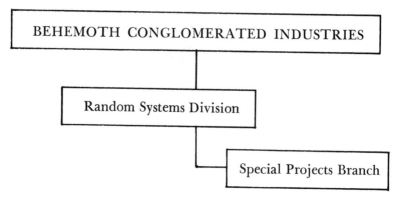

Figure 10. The First Spin-Off

organization chart will be the freewheeling pursuit of ideas about ordinal randomness. No higher executive will have authority to impose Now demands on the Special Projects Branch. It will be Behemoth's in-house think tank in the field of random systems.

Naturally, the new branch will spin off from Taskwright's Random Systems Division.

The bureaucratic result of priority splitting is, in scientific terms, the *Spin-Off Effect:*

The Functions of a System Lost in End-Means Inversion Are Recovered in a New System.

The Front-Parlor Effect

The clearest illustration of how the Spin-Off Effect works in organizations lies in a domestic analogy. In days gone by, the living room was the place where a family literally "lived," where it came together when it was not otherwise occupied in kitchen, bedroom, or bath. Today houses are still built with living rooms but rare is the family that actually lives in one. In some households family members are barred from the living room, which has become the equivalent of the Victorian front parlor alternating as a furniture museum and a reception room for guests of higher social status. In a few households not even guests are permitted in the living room, despite its plastic slip covers. In some cases families have actually cordoned off their living rooms with velvet ropes. The white shag carpeting will bear no traffic at all. One may look but not touch.

After the living room became a museum, its social functions reappeared in other rooms. In many homes warm, roomy kitchens have become the family social center. In others it is a basement recreation room. Still others employ a spare bedroom as a den or television room.

In more recent construction an entirely new room has been invented to absorb the activities banned from the living room: the *family room.*

Nevertheless, living rooms are still being built in modern homes. As a result, the costs of housing, energy and furnishings are higher than necessary because we build more space than we use. As it is with suburban houses, so it is with organizations.

The Spin-Off Observed

Before World War I the hiring and training of workers in American factories was part of the production supervisor's job. During the war, factories were forced to work beyond capacity. Supervisors, burdened by the Now demands of production, no longer had time for the Later tasks of interviewing prospective employees and teaching beginners. The result has been the widespread Spin-Off of personnel departments to do the hiring and training chronically left undone by first line managers.

American universities, once believed immune to the foibles that afflict less cloistered institutions, have not escaped the Spin-Off Effect. Originally, the university was a sanctuary where scholars retreated from worldly affairs to think. Today, however, university professors must endure the distractions of attending committee meetings, grading papers, directing theses, and planning new courses. As a result, the only way a university can free scholars for introspection, not only from the clamor of the outside world but also from the bureaucratic demands of the university itself, is by spinning off a Center for Advanced Thought.

Planning commissions are a common feature of municipal governments. But planning is inherently a Later type of work. Few indeed are the planning boards that do any planning at all. On the contrary, they are besieged by the Now demands of petitions for zoning variances and construction permits. Spin-Off inventions such as Citizens Advisory Committees have sprung up to do the planning the planners can't get to.

Long ago the Trendy Heights school system abandoned

reading, writing, and arithmetic for courses in Driver Education, Self-Expression, and Adjustment to Contemporary Life. When some of the parents finally rebelled and demanded that the schools instill at least literacy and mathematical competence, the school administration established a Basic Education Workshop for a select 10 percent of the students. Visions of multiplication tables and the classics danced in the heads of appeased parents. The Basic Education Workshop appeared as a Spin-Off system, housed in temporary buildings and taught by older teachers who weren't sufficiently familiar with modular curriculum programming, audiovisual scheduling, or experiential enrichment to be of much use to the prevailing system. The Spin-Off unit captured the original purpose lost by the school system.

The Informal Spin-Off

There is a variety of Spin-Off, especially common in government, in which no clearly visible office appears to adopt an abandoned function. This does not mean that the function goes unperformed. Instead, an informal arrangement does the job.*

Lyndon Johnson, realizing the inability of his White House staff to assess the conflict in Vietnam, went to Washington attorneys Dean Acheson and Clark Clifford. Jimmy Carter turned to his friend, Atlanta lawyer Charles Kirbo, in moments of crisis. Richard Nixon consulted Bebe Rebozo about God knows what.

Peace is now too important to be left to the designated peacemakers. While every military conflict leads to an obli-

---

* At least in the beginning. If the informal arrangement works, someone is sure to love it enough to organize it. There is no denying the Organizing Trap.

gatory peace conference in Paris or Geneva, these gatherings are relics whose usefulness hasn't been apparent since before the Versailles Treaty of 1919. Without exception, the real settlement is made elsewhere, in informal meetings between negotiators, out of sight of press and public.

Sometimes an *Informal Spin-Off* is embodied in nothing more than a casual social encounter. Witness the standard military briefing, which lost its substance long ago. There are few things—even in the military—that consume so much energy with so few results as a command briefing.

Before the eyes of visiting brass, military hosts project a somatic succession of statistics, justifications, and charts onto a screen. Junior officers doodle while awaiting their turns to deliver tediously rehearsed talks.

In the meantime, a high-ranking guest, the sole audience for this business, reads teletype messages, scribbles notes, and whispers instructions to an aide, who slips in and out of the room. The one thing the VIP never does is look at the screen. He doesn't have to. He already has staple-bound facsimile copies of each speech and slide.

These audiovisual presentations haven't communicated anything in years. How, then, is information conveyed? In casual conversation over lunch, at a cocktail reception in the officers' club, or in the staff car on the way to the airport. That's where the general turns to his host and asks, "Now, colonel, what the hell do you people out here really need to get this damned project off the ground?"

The Inversion Corollary

Once Later tasks have been displaced by Now jobs, busy managers can never retrieve them in their own jobs. A department that has gone astray simply cannot get back on the track to its original destination. This harsh truth is stated as the *Inversion Corollary:*

Once Ends and Means Have Inverted, They Can Never Switch Back.

Resisting the Corollary leads to irrational behavior. Only imperceptive executives exhort their subordinates to tackle the Later work. Sermonizing about how busy people can always find time for important things solves nothing.

The Ins and Outs of Spin-Offs

If a task is vital, it will get done. But, as the Inversion Corollary instructs us, that task will never get done by the department that didn't do it in the first place.

A new entity must arise.

At Behemoth Conglomerated, the Special Projects Branch was spawned as a dependent of the Random Systems Division. It was an *Internal Spin-Off.* But there is also the *External Spin-Off,* in which an outside system springs up to pursue the lost ends.

Consider the final state of obedience training for dogs in Whistlehalt. As a result of its End-Means Inversion the Whistlehalt Obedience Club abandoned dog training altogether in favor of running the club. Two members, disgruntled over the club's inability to train dogs, quit and brought together an informal, unorganized group of puppy owners on a cooperative basis.

The training sessions take place in the same supermarket parking lot where the established Whistlehalt Obedience Club began long ago. This new little group is an External Spin-Off, recovering the purposes lost by the Whistlehalt Obedience Club.

Busy managers cannot get their undone Later tasks off the

back burner. A Spin-Off auxiliary is imperative. It's the only way to recapture lost purposes.

External Spin-Offs happen in business as well. Originally, Howard Johnson's Motor Lodges and Holiday Inns offered simple accommodations at low rates. Soon enough they evolved into elaborate pleasure domes replete with swimming pools, gourmet menus, saunas, and rates to match. The idea of thrifty accommodations, too good to be lost, was recouped by an External Spin-Off, the "Motel 6" concept, offering austere rooms at low rates.

How long before color TVs and ankle-deep carpeting appear in Motel 6? How long before entrepreneurs who own Motel 6's realize that Mobil five-star restaurants attract business? How long before they compete for the role of local civic center by adding meeting rooms, intimate bars, and Fundomes?

Not very.

Chapter 14

The Spin-Off Corollaries

How the Spin-Off Keeps Spinning

Life is just one damn thing after another.
—Frank Ward O'Malley

Lockstep Bootery, cited by a consumer protection agency for manufacturing children's shoe soles from flammable foam rubber, sought to avoid the embarrassment and expense of a protracted legal battle. Settling for a consent decree saved legal fees but accomplished only half of the purpose. As so often happens, technical innocence left the unmistakable appearance of guilt.

To reverse the initial trickle of bad press and protect the company's good name, Lockstep hired Hornblower to take charge of its beefed-up public-relations department.

In no time Hornblower was stuffing executive in-baskets with weekly reports on the number of press releases sent out, newspaper column inches garnered, radio scripts distributed, TV film clips mailed, minutes of broadcast air time logged, interview shows booked and talks arranged by a new Speakers Bureau.

Hornblower had wrapped himself in comfortable Now tasks. But all his frenzied activity did nothing to rescue Lockstep, whose sales continued to drop. Management wanted results; its PR director gave them only statistics. At first, management mistook Hornblower's numbers for results. They had no idea that he had transformed an unstructured crisis into a set of convenient routines.

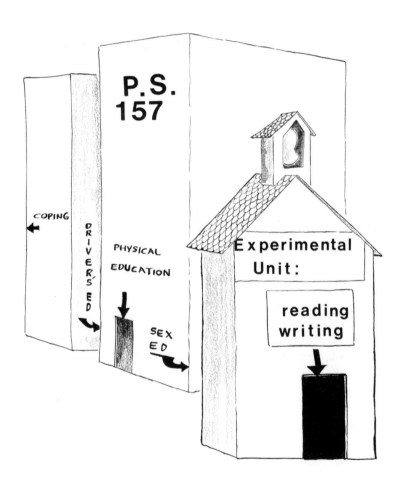

As the crisis deepened, however, Lockstep's executives realized that Hornblower's PR shop was saving neither the company's image nor its share of the market. No one was quicker to agree than Hornblower himself, who pleaded for additional aides.

Lockstep's anxious management went along. A new PR unit, the Emergency Corporate Communications Office (ECCO), was spun off. Puffman, a publicist renowned for creativity and aggressiveness, was put in charge. The purposes lost in the bustle and shuffle of Hornblower's PR department went to Puffman's crisis center.

The Spin-Off Keeps Spinning

Puffman, however, proved no more able than Hornblower to resist the temptation to reduce uncertainty. He too fell prey to the Priority Split. ECCO succumbed to sorting and counting all manner of activities previously believed beyond quantification.*

Still Lockstep's sales figures plummeted. An overworked Puffman recommended the creation of a special image-building task force reporting to ECCO.

Thus was born the Public Affairs Project (PAP). Flack was lured away from a stylish little advertising agency to be the team leader.

Meanwhile, Behemoth Conglomerated Industries acquired Lockstep just in time to rescue it from financial collapse brought on by excessive administrative overhead and a deteriorating public image. A month before the takeover, however, a national business magazine ran a feature on the sophistication of Lockstep's PR operation.

The mischievous phenomenon described here is known in

---

* Puffman had an MA in social psychology, which explains his propensity to assign numbers to the incalculable.

scholarly circles as the *First Spin-Off Corollary:*

A Succession of Spin-Offs Will Evolve as Each in Turn Loses the Purposes Inherited from the One Before.

The First Corollary at Work

Back at the Random Systems Division, the Special Projects Branch couldn't digest the ambiguities of its open-ended goals. Shielded from corporate schedules and routines, Special Projects created its own regularities. It scheduled project completion dates, issued interim progress reports, generated expense justifications, and published a monthly bulletin, *Recent Developments in Ordinal Randomness.*

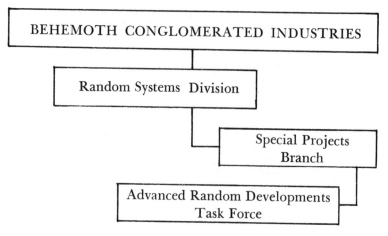

Figure 11. Second-order Spin-Off

Special Projects bustled about consuming salaries, overtime pay, consulting fees, travel funds, furnishing allowances, printing costs, and subscription fees. It bustled so much, in fact, that it had no time for the spontaneous study of ordinal randomness, the Later work for which it had been created.

Again Behemoth fell behind in technical knowledge.

Again somebody upstairs came down.

Again the bosses found that the people responsible for developing ordinal randomness were too busy *administering* the development of ordinal randomness.

Again Now had pushed Later, first to the back burner, then right off the stove.

Again the company solved an organization problem in the only way it knew.

Thus it came to pass that Behemoth Conglomerated set up its Advanced Random Developments Task Force, which

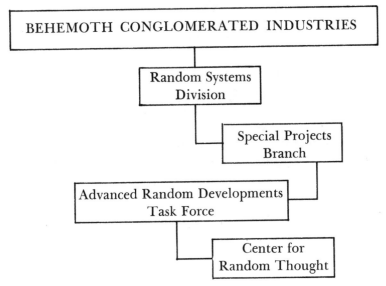

Figure 12. Third-order Spin-Off

reported to the Special Projects Branch, which, in turn, still answered to the Random Systems Division. Attentive students of organization should not be shocked to learn that two and a half years later the overworked Advanced Random Developments Task Force spun off a Center for Random Thought. The disease had become an epidemic.

The Labor Theory of Value

Why wasn't Taskwright given a pink slip instead of a Special Projects Branch?

Why weren't Hornblower and Puffman sent to the unemployment lines when Flack came in to do what they couldn't?

Why does a system which has lost its way survive to go on eating resources while its work is assigned to Spin-Offs?

Rare is the executive who will eliminate a department merely because it no longer does what it is supposed to do. Adhering to the Labor Theory of Value,* the managerial mind reasons that even a redundant office must be doing something worthwhile if it simply looks busy.

The Labor Theory of Value is alive and well outside the world of markets and prices. Indeed, it is thriving. Economics honors graduates, who could destroy the Theory in three good sentences, will nonetheless embrace it when called upon to run an organization. Few can resist its common sense: being busy is a virtue unto itself quite apart from whether benefits result.

The occasional executive who doubts the usefulness of a department will find himself buried in justifications, rationalizations, and dog and pony shows defending the office's indispensability.

---

* The oldest and certainly the most intuitive of value notions, the Labor Theory of Value holds that "labour alone is . . . the ultimate and real standard by which all commodities can . . . be estimated and compared" (Adam Smith, 1776). It was the foundation of Classical and much Socialist economic thought.

The Second Corollary

The Police Department in Regiment City has never been larger, its pay higher, or its equipment more elaborate. Yet industrialists, merchants, and neighborhood associations must hire private guards to protect their factories, their homes, and themselves.

If you are robbed in Regiment City, a police car will reach you within seven minutes of a call. Regiment City's finest will ask questions, furrow their brows, tip back their hats, scribble notes, and fill out forms.

But this is not protection. The RCPD still gobbles up resources, but it is doing something entirely different from what we think a police department does.

Why, then, is the Police Department still around? First, the police force *may be* a deterrent to crime. Who knows but that strollers might get mugged twice as often if there were no police?

Second, and more important, is the iron grip of Haga's Law. The Police Department's presence is a comforting factor. Not having the police around would breed anxiety. Police brass, politicians, and ultimately the voters will leave nothing to chance.

As new systems spin off from existing organizations, they leave in their wake an accumulation of Priority Split ancestors that consume much and contribute little. This eventuality is known as the *Second Spin-Off Corollary:*

Systems That Lose Their Purposes Are Never Abolished.

A Skeleton in the Cabinet

The presidential Cabinet began extra-constitutionally under George Washington to advise him. Early presidents had no full-time professional aides save an occasional clerk or messenger. The Cabinet secretaries were, in effect, both administrative assistants to the president and the managers of government departments.

By the 1930s administrative detail had so burdened the Cabinet that President Roosevelt formed a "Kitchen Cabinet" of personal advisers to do what formal Cabinet officers no longer could. Today the Cabinet has lost substance and purpose.

Where, then, did the functions of coordination, policy formulation, and governmental supervision go? To the descendants of Roosevelt's Kitchen Cabinet, that pack of special assistants for this and special counselors for that who occupy the White House in ever-growing numbers. This army of functionaries is now a counterpart in miniature of the entire executive branch. Predictably, the White House staff has so burdened itself with preparing position papers, news summaries, and impact statements that recent presidents must seek personal advisers elsewhere.

Nevertheless, neither the Cabinet nor the White House staff gives any indication that they will disappear just because they have lost their advisory function.

Is There No End to It?

Inside the Ministry of War, supply bureaus employ thousands of people and consume billions of dollars. Yet long ago they ceased to be a reliable source of military supplies. In peacetime such bureaucratic impotence is little more than an irritation. In battle the failure of the supply system is a downright hazard.

During the last war, the Logistics Command circumvented the stagnant supply system by spinning off the Red Express System to expedite rush orders. Red Express promised to deliver vital aircraft parts and combat equipment to front-line units within twenty-four hours. This worked until the managers of Red Express, falling prey to the Priority Split, worked vigorously on administering the system rather than rushing orders.

Soon enough the laudable twenty-four-hour delivery service slipped to thirty hours. Then to thirty-six. When it took the better part of two weeks to deliver, say, an artillery-aiming computer module, high-level commanders noticed that Red Express had become as slow as the conventional methods it was designed to bypass.

The brass did the only thing for which their training had prepared them. They supplemented the ineffective Red Express with another logistical wonder, the Blue Dart Program. Blue Dart promised to deliver vital material to the war zone within twenty-four hours.

And so it goes. Spin-Offs keep spinning seemingly without end, leaving behind them dormant systems that can't do what they should. In the meantime, an organization gets administratively fatter as it loses its way and tries to find it again. The end comes only when a system's resources are spread too thin. And every effort to fix an over-organized system through successive Spin-Offs only hastens the decline.

Chapter 15

The Hierarchitecture Hypothesis

How Fortress Bureaucracy Is Built

Out of this nettle, danger, we pluck this flower, safety.
—*Henry IV, Part I*

For all their talk about being open and responsive to their environments, systems everywhere are anxious to close their organizational drapes against the outside world.

For all their talk about community orientation and responsiveness to the needs of society, organizations, as a matter of course, shutter their windows and pull up their institutional drawbridges.

They Deserve a Breakloop Today

The outside world is a Pandora's Box of stimulation, threats, criticism, and demands.

Unveil a three-function digital watch for seventy dollars and the market demands five functions for thirty dollars.

Solve the problem of racial bias in hiring and the environment brings up sexist bias in promoting.

Handle a sales crisis here and a production crisis breaks out there.

Satisfy blue-collar wage demands and the white-collar union clamors to top them.

As birds keep an eye on cats and cats are wary of dogs, even the newest and simplest organizations soon enough recognize their natural enemy: the environment around them. The outside world will leave an organization no peace. No

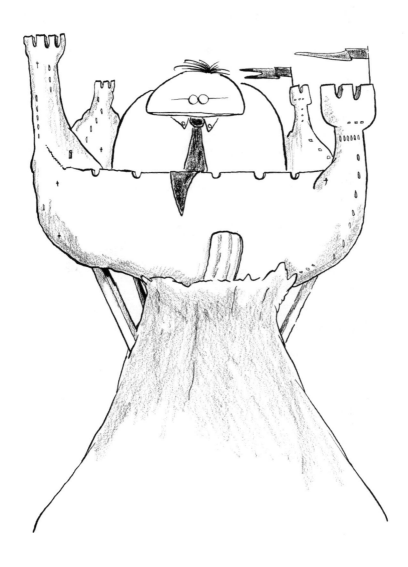

sooner does a warm little group—say, the Through Channels Sailing Club—devise a sprinkling of specialization or add a dash of hierarchy then it runs into forces prodding it to do some things better, do others differently, and stop doing a few altogether. There is no end to it.

Small wonder that people who work in organizations want the world to go away. Just when they imagine they deserve a short rest on their laurels, the outside world, ungrateful for past efforts, wants them back on their toes again. Only an extraordinary personality can survive a diet of constant stimulation and unbroken effort.

As Figure 13 illustrates, .the shape of a new system matches its environment.

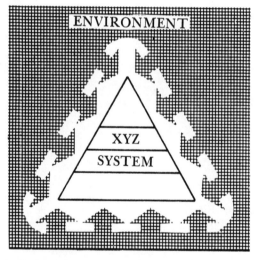

Figure 13. System Structure Matches Environment Forces

But having built the system once, managers are loath to keep changing. In the meantime, as Figure 14 depicts, the environment keeps changing, gradually but persistently. This process continues until the old structure is so out of phase with its surroundings that it no longer works. Crisis

Figure 14.
System Structure Sufficiently Mismatched with Environment
Forces to Destroy System Function in Inevitable Crisis

is upon it and collapse is the result. (See Figure 15.) From
the crisis will emerge a new structure, if any structure sur-
vives at all. (See Figure 16.)

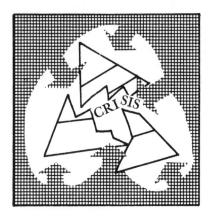

Figure 15.
System Structure Unchanged while Environment Forces
Drift Further Out of Phase

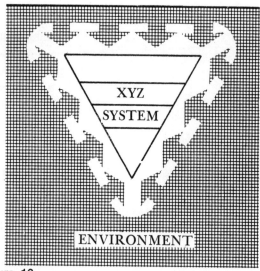

Figure 16.
Optimist's Consolation: Out of Crisis a New System Is
Formed with Structure Matching Current Environment Forces

The Breakloop Apparent Exception

Breakloops are the envy of Demand Loop systems. Seemingly, Breakloops can ignore irksome environments forever. Indeed, they get their organization groceries delivered year after year without paying heed to nagging outside elements.

Yet not even the apparently impregnable Breakloop defenses actually work forever. Observant students well know that since environments are in flux and Breakloops stand still, Breakloops drift out of phase with their surroundings. Finally, even well-insulated Breakloops reach a critical mismatch with their environments. The Breakloop organization then crashes into the very elements it had so long avoided.

Feedback loops may be broken, but environments do not go away. Breakloop insulation merely delays the inevitable. It does not prevent collision with reality.

Crimping the Loop

Unshielded Demand Loops, in the meantime, must contend with environmental stimuli by making repeated adjustments. Demand Loops hunger for the Breakloops' isolation from the irritations of the outside world. They yearn to escape their environments. If annoying feedback loops cannot be cut, they surely can be crimped. A day rarely passes that a Demand Loop organization does not take some step to shield itself from the press of encompassing elements.

Corporations, the most highly organized Demand Loop systems, are ever busy absorbing markets and suppliers. Few things reduce Demand Loop exposure to risk as much as absorbing customers and suppliers into a corporate family.

Demand Loops screen themselves from the fickle oscillation of their markets by franchising retailers, invoking "fair trade" prices, seeking government-regulated route allocations, or declaring themselves "natural" monopolies requiring legal prohibition of competitors. Licensing, professional standards boards, and bans on advertising do much the same thing. Labor relations are made predictable by moving operations to regions where local culture discourages unions. If these moves are insufficient to shelter a company from environing winds, corporations resort to government contracts, thereby constructing for themselves quasi-Breakloop protection against the ups and downs of selling to the private sector.

In the early days of the iron horse, railroads in the eastern United States were vexed by small lines that cut prices and took better care of the freight. These eastern lines lobbied for the Interstate Commerce Commission to regulate their new competitors out of business. Public regulation is a popular way to crimp Demand Loop feedback.

Before deregulation US airlines did much the same thing as the railroads. Preferring to rest on their laurels rather than rouse themselves to price competition, they settled in behind a Civil Aeronautics Board. While the CAB controlled air fares and allocated routes, the airlines carried on a pretense of competition through in-flight entertainment, baggage handling races, and designer-garbed cabin attendants.

Foul Uncertainty

Prices, voters, suppliers, customers, constituents, clients, bosses, governing boards, competitors, and new ideas conspire to keep systems—Breakloops and Demand Loops alike —off balance. Outside elements are the infectious carriers of uncertainty's fever. If these circumjacent powers can be ignored, even the slightest bit, all systems can take a break today.

Getting rid of uncertainty is axiomatically a good thing. Certainty is the bedrock of rational decisions, a prerequisite to long-range planning and the mother of efficiency. Mankind, therefore, organizes to make predictable what was once chaotic.

Bite-Sized Chunks

Organized systems head off environmental perils with the only means they know—the one method that unfailingly quelled surprises before—*Organize Away the Threat*.

Faced with a big, undefined, whelming environment, managers have learned to take what they cannot swallow whole and break it down into bite-sized chunks. What a system would have choked on before, it can now digest with ease, piece by piece. Organizations everywhere chop and dice the totality of the outside world into wieldy categories called *Subenvironments*.

Organizations meet each piece of subenvironment one on

one with a specialized staff of experts. Threats from the financial subenvironment are watched and countered by a Finance Department. The chances of being surprised by a competitor's technological breakthrough are reduced by setting up a Research and Development staff. The ebb and flow of customers' tastes are monitored and tested by a Market Research Department.

Precarious College, dependent upon gifts for financial survival, naturally sees donors as an awesome outside force. No one can be dismayed, then, to learn that the Precarious faculty is smaller than the college's staff of fund raisers. Moreover, this staff subdivides its donor environment and assigns each chunk to a staff specialist. One oversees mail solicitation, another arranges the annual Save Precarious dinner dance, and a third solicits deferred gifts from alumni.

Bisibee, president of Backdoor Corporation, was so distracted by a constant parade of minor crises that he appointed a special assistant in charge of what a press release called "day-to-day, short-fuse, externally generated problems." Faced with a hodgepodge of minor troubles from no particular subenvironment, a system may simply lump them into a new category: miscellaneous.

Staffing Up

Long ago Snapback Girdle and Truss, threatened by rumors of a technical breakthrough in two-way elastics, created a Research and Development Department. Today virtually all organizations have one.

Trauma Casualty of Hartford, anticipating a "go-go" era in insurance marketing, gained an edge over competitors by setting up a New Lines Department.

Similarly, the advertising firm of Bibb & Tucker assigned a senior partner to work exclusively on the vital matter of "new business."

Corporations far and wide have created formal jobs for futurists—specialists in an allegedly scientific approach to crystal-ball gazing. Gillette Razor, Shell Oil, General Electric, and American Telephone & Telegraph have them; others cannot be far behind.

The Hypothesis Divulged

The compelling practice of building scanning departments to watch unpredictable subenvironments has been formulated as the *Hierarchitecture Hypothesis:* *

An Organization Will Build a Staff at the Point Where a Threat Is Greatest.

* In their *Organizations* (John Wiley & Sons, 1958), James March and Nobel laureate Herbert Simon revealed that the division of labor among staffs was almost a mirror image of differences between environment elements. It was Mason Haire, in his *Modern Organization Theory* (John Wiley & Sons, 1959), who gave the Law of Staffs its present formulation, using a shelf-bracket metaphor: a brace is strongest where the force tending to destroy it is greatest. He devised the Law, however, in a study of threats that arose *inside* organizations. This is its first application to *external* perils.

Chapter 16

The Fat,
Happy, and Dumb Process

The Environment's Gonna Gitcha

What boots it at one gate to make defence
And at another to let in the foe?
—John Milton

Since organizations see outside threats coming from every direction, they are soon larded with staffs, all presumably bustling and scanning their own subenvironments. Thus, the attempt to detect surprises and defend against threats adds to the bulk of an organization's administrative overhead. This is a first step in a process elegantly described as *Fat, Happy, and Dumb.*

Fat

In days long gone, the Big Three American carmakers evolved a technique for minimizing the bother of watching the outside world. Each defined the environment as a tidy entity: the Other Two.

The hazard in watching for outside perils was shockingly obvious once the industry had been surprised by Ralph Nader's aggressive consumerism.

The Motor City was still reeling from Nader's attacks when it was hit by the Arab oil boycott.

Today the American auto industry gushes with sensitivity to the environment. Recognizing remote dangers at every

hand, the Big Three have fallen to dealing with unpredictable forces in the only way known to mankind. Organizing Threats Away. Indeed, General Motors has set up a Societal Research Department staffed with sociologists and psychologists.

Thus, the first and predictable *Fat* step has been taken.

Happy

Coverwell Thread and Yarn did a thriving business manufacturing the yarn used in baseballs.

Coverwell hired Clearsight to head the new Market Research Department. Clearsight, in turn, hired a statistician to look at population figures, an international affairs specialist to estimate baseball's appeal on other continents, a sociologist to examine the effect of women's liberation on baseball equipment sales, a lawyer to follow the sports news, and a retired left fielder to lobby with the Baseball Commissioner's Office. Clearsight had fortified Coverwell with an army of professional scouts to watch the outside world. Having covered all the bases, so to speak, Clearsight lapsed into the contented state we call *Happy.*

Managers who indulge the conceit that they are shielded from surprise are merely insulated against bad news. The point at which they imagine they have the environment under control is the very moment when they are most vulnerable to its caprices. The Fat and Happy steps—administrative obesity and managerial stupor respectively—combine to expose an organization even more to enveloping dangers.

Dumb

Just as the bosses upstairs in the hierarchy are lulled by the thought that they have the best environment specialists money can buy, those specialists start to do something else. They may start with open-ended, unprogrammed Later tasks.

But nothing will be left to chance. The scanners fear that just watching and tossing ideas around won't pass muster. How, they wonder, can the bosses upstairs evaluate their worth if they do no work that is measurable, tangible, visible, and, above all, quantifiable? Alack, the staff specialists who are supposed to be ranging far and wide looking for a trend here, a tendency there, fall to churning out reports, devising programs, and putting up window dressing as testimony to their indispensability.

Now work pushes out unprogrammed Later tasks.

Means become ends.

The bosses have carefully built Fortress Bureaucracy, but the people hired to watch from its parapets bend their heads over desks preparing interim progress reports. They construct routine where none existed and none was needed.

Coverwell's statistician grew preoccupied with reports on how he planned to overcome inaccuracies in census data. The lawyer fell to summarizing Supreme Court precedents for baseball's antitrust exemption. And the old left fielder became consumed with trying to figure out his monthly expense account.

With no one watching, the environment inevitably sneaks up on an unwary organization. While the drawbridge is up, the back door is ajar. While outside forces move along without halt—raising a threat here, offering an opportunity there —nobody is telling top management what is going on. The expert watchmen are out to lunch. Ergo, the final *Dumb* phase that follows Fat and Happy in obscuring signals from the outside world.

The Shock Zone

The confusion and dismay generated by the Dumb phase of organizational staffing up against uncertainty are depicted in Figure 17. The left half of the graph looks very much

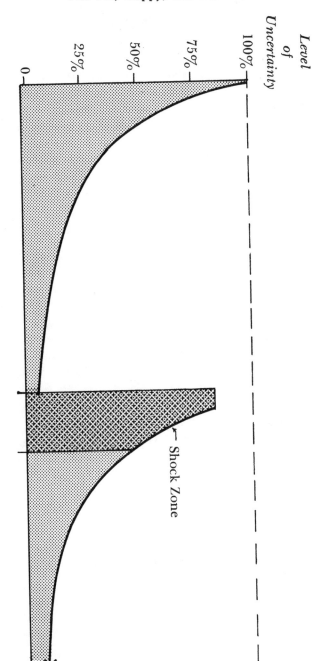

Figure 17. The Shock Zone of the Dumb Stage.

like Figure 1 in Chapter 1 which, of course, it is. That part of the graph between 0 and Point N is immediately recognizable as the First Propensity that comprises Haga's Law: *Anxiety Begets Organizing.* Each added step in the organizing process reduces the level of anxiety. Then the Potato Chip Imperative sets in, and the process becomes a mad pursuit of the last breath of uncertainty. However, as the vigilant reader can perceive, more organizing piled atop more organizing shaves the level of happenstance by thinner and thinner increments. Yet, the Imperative-crazed organizers appear to redouble their pursuit of what is becoming progressively and swiftly unattainable: the erasure of the last trace of uncertainty. Deep into the clutches of their futile obsession with elusive small threats, managers are rendered deaf and blind to the big threats all around.

As administrators push environ-scanning further into formality, rules, reports, and procedures, a system must finally be organized right up to Point N.* At Point N, the sky falls. The unwatched environment springs an inevitable surprise. The right half of Figure 17 shows the Second Propensity's unanticipated mischief: *Organizing Begets Anxiety.* At Point N, the level of uncertainty in the system is driven back up to frightening heights, despite the Byzantine complexity that has grown precisely to whittle down the system's vulnerability to chance and hazard. Gone is the security that the system had bought with its bloated staffs of environment watchers.

Between the moment of surprise at Point N and some later point, which is approximated by Point R,† the stricken system reels in shock and puzzlement. Not knowing what else

---

* The N stands for Nader (as in Ralph) in memory of his surprise to an organization and an industry—both of which considered themselves well staffed against surprises.

† The R represents Recovery, the point where further organizing again brings down the level of uncertainty. Point R for General Motors was the establishment of the Societal Research Department.

to do in its state of crisis, it does what it has already learned well enough to do: it keeps on organizing still more.* At Point R, administrators regain their sea legs and begin to pull the system out of shock. As before, they discover that a little more organizing cuts down on a whole lot of uncertainty. And, again, they pursue that linear fallacy right into the ground. The history of the left half of Figure 17 will be repeated on the right half. Having learned nothing from one scare, organizers plunge back into the sweaty pursuit of diminishing unpredictability. Unswervingly, further seizures of anxiety-aversion will fling them into yet another Point N. It can be no other way. How many rounds of this irresistable process an organization can absorb (if indeed it can survive even one environmental jack-in-the-box) remains to be seen.

The Axiom Expressed

The lesson of the Fat, Happy, and Dumb process has been put into the words of science as *Acocella's Axiom:*

The More an Organization Staffs to Scan Its Environment, the Less It Sees.

Surprise

The malevolent Fat, Happy, and Dumb process is unavoidable. Not even large and thoroughly staffed systems can escape its universal seduction.

When military conscription was ended, the Army set about learning to merchandise its virtues to eighteen-year-olds. The Army's best minds focused on raising pay, improv-

---

* Chapter 17, which follows, deals with the organizing response to crisis in greater scientific detail.

ing training, upgrading leadership, and making life attractive in a green uniform. Even the Army's detractors confessed that it made progress on these fronts. Unfortunately, while the Army was learning to sell itself, no one in the system scanned population statistics. By the late 1970s, eighteen-year-olds had become a scarce commodity in the United States.

The Army, at least, can excuse its oversight. Population projections, after all, are not its primary business. That sort of expertise is believed to dwell in Academe. It falls to scholars to contemplate the future and probe the social environment.

But scholars, too, were caught napping by the drop in the birthrate. Higher education had erected monumental physical plants and had overstaffed to cope with the consequences of the World War II baby boom. The academics were, however, gulled by the fallacy of linear thinking. If the country was whelmed by young people in the 1960s, they reasoned, it would be whelmed by them forever. At Mutchadoo State University, which could afford such things, an Office of Long-Range Planning and Analysis was established to project past trends linearly into the future.

In the early 1970s, when the World War II crop of babies matured into adulthood, leaving behind a dearth of college-aged people, few were as astonished as academics, society's full-time, professional staff of environment scanners. The very group that should have had its eye on the environment didn't. It cannot be any other way.

Fatter Still

Atloss was promoted to the new post of director of Technical Affairs for Titanic Shipping, Ltd., with the bare mandate to keep abreast of what competitors were doing with containerization. Atloss's job was, clearly, industrial espionage, an enterprise unfettered by task structure or paperwork routines. Atloss had a free hand to do a job that he alone knew how to do.

But a free hand soon binds itself. As director of Technical Affairs, Atloss spoke before Titanic's Annual Staff Performance Review Committee, made up of the company's vicepresidents and chaired by the chief executive officer. Atloss's report, entitled "The Year in Technical Affairs," poured out statistics on the number of professional meetings attended, man-hours expended, papers published, and dollars spent. Atloss also anesthetized his audience with a comprehensive recital of the abstracts of each technical paper prepared by the staff during the year. Most of their titles had to do with "statistical models of optimum cargo routes." The review committee, however, had expected Atloss to reveal what Titanic's competitors were doing about cargo-handling systems.

Atloss's presentation to the committee was interrupted by a message that a rival firm, Magellan-Lisbon Lines, was building a new fleet of container ships using a revolutionary twin-hulled design. It was the first that the Titanic executives had heard of such a thing. Surprise!

Preventive Spin-Off

Astute observers will know at once that Titanic Shipping had been lured into a Fat, Happy, and Dumb trap. Believing that Atloss had been watching the environment, the company's leaders were understandably astonished to discover that no one had been watching it. Atloss had been driving uncertainty out of his job by turning it into a comfortable, structured set of Now deadlines.

Shaken by environmental shock, the corporate leaders at Titanic could only act to make sure it didn't happen again. The ready solution in all such cases is the commonsense

Preventive Spin-Off. Believing that its Technical Affairs Department was otherwise overburdened, Titanic spun off a special new subunit, the Technical Awareness Branch. The company invested its new TAB with but one purpose: monitor engineering developments among Titanic's competitors. This, of course, had been the Technical Affairs Department's original objective, before Atloss fell prey to the Priority Split and elevated quantifiable distractions into major aims. When a specialist staff fails to keep up with its assigned subenvironment, then its scanning job is shifted to a newly organized appendage.

Spin Again

As students of organizational perversity will predict, a new environment-scanning department, with unprogrammed work to do, must unswervingly routinize. Seymour, the new director of Technical Awareness, will be no more able than his scanning predecessor, Atloss, to digest ambiguous duties. TAB will go the way of TAD, down the path of least anxiety to daily routine and calculable output.

Again the environment will go unwatched.

Again the organization will be caught by surprise.

And again the Spin-Off process will be repeated.

Over-Spinning

The number of body blows a system can absorb from its environment cannot be predicted with accuracy. The factors are many and complicated. Surely, however, enough surprises must lead to one too many.

Titanic Shipping, Ltd., found that what had obtained when TAB spun off from TAD was only the beginning. Before long the company's headquarters staff of environment scanners was larger than its operating management. Simultaneously, its knowledge of outside forces was lost in a mountain of monthly statistical reports. Administrative overhead costs rose while shipping revenues plummeted. The company was subsequently sold, at a heavy discount, to Behemoth Conglomerated Industries.

An Irresistible Process

Every effort to organize away the unpredictability of the outside world results in Priority Split. Mankind's loathing of uncertainty makes this inevitable. Acocella's Axiom cannot be escaped.

Even knowing that their appointed guards are likely to fall asleep in the parapet, managers have no choice but to keep on organizing. Faced with threats from uncertain quarters, they must augment their staffs. The outside world is fraught with danger. A manager must anticipate it, watch it, cushion its impact, absorb its punch. Managers are paid to act. Not to act is to leave things to chance.

Nothing will be left to chance.

Chapter 17
Crisis Crystallization

How Emergencies Beget Administrative Monuments

. . . all our troubles proceed from their being unexpected.
—Plutarch

When the Ministry of Forests's annual budget was pruned by 10 percent, it convened a cost-cutting advisory committee that soon published a *Cost Slasher Bulletin.*

When a driver employed by Klutz Trucking Company backed a semitrailer over an unseen Volkswagen, the city council of Regiment Park decreed that thereafter all backing trucks must be preceded by a flagman.

Even the smallest disasters are quickly doctored with administrative quackeries. The managerial Band-Aid or legislative poultice, applied in the sweat of emergency, crystallizes into a durable hindrance to getting things done.

A frenzied form of the well-known Shiftscheme Response is the haven of every administrator trapped in the jaws of crisis.

Froth of Calamity

Certainly there are cases where measures taken in a time of turmoil have dampened crisis and alleviated distress. But far more common are instances in which the "rescue" bears

no relationship to the predicament. Worse still are those instances in which the remedy is memorialized in committees, projects, controls, departments, rules, jobs, forms, and reports.

At no time is bureaucracy expanded with greater abandon than during emergencies. Few administrators can foresee that decisions taken in the heat of battle today will congeal into bureaucratic burdens tomorrow.

The untutored will ask how bureaucracy—a creation of patient rationalization—can be built at all in the froth of calamity. The answer is that organizations act to survive. What an administrative hierarchy calls a crisis is actually an environmental surprise.

Not a Drop to Drink

The Kingdom of Boravia was suffering its third year of drought. During question time in Parliament, the opposition leader demanded of the government, "What steps are being taken to end the drought?" On the face of it, nothing could be done. The matter was in the hands of God and the prevailing westerly winds.

But the Prime Minister of Boravia could not blurt out such a confession. To do so would manifest an impolitic indifference to the plight of the people. The opposition leader would relish such an admission and use it to bring down the government. For that reason—and for scarcely any others —the Prime Minister could not utter the only realistic answer.

The pressure of circumstances compelled the Prime Minister to look the opposition leader in the eye and reply that the government does, indeed, have a program for ending the drought. "I shall announce it to the nation on Sunday in a special television speech." The next few days will be consumed in devising a crash program to do what is clearly impossible.

The Crisis Criteria

We have observed this malignant process in a host of cases. The fruits of our endeavors are the criteria by which capable students may judge whether a response to bureaucratic distress is morally and politically acceptable.

CRITERION 1: SOMETHING MUST BE DONE.

CRITERION 2: IT MUST BE DONE NOW.

CRITERION 3: IT MUST BE DONE FOR ALL TO SEE.

Criterion 1: Something Must Be Done

In an emergency, *not* to "do something" is morally unthinkable. Something must always be done. Refusing to act in the smoke of crisis is to leave things to chance.

CRISIS CASE X-1: THE BORAVIAN WATERGATES

As part of the Prime Minister's program to solve the Great Boravian Drought, the Royal Water Utility (RWU) distributed hollow plastic devices to its customers. These devices were said to reduce the volume of water consumed in flushing toilets. The Royal Water Utility assumed that when the so-called watergates were used throughout the kingdom, water consumption would decrease.

A letter published in the *Times of Boravia* revealed that bending the float valve rod in the toilet tank would also save water. Such mechanical common sense, however, had no place in the RWU's scheme. The utility's problem—and the Prime Minister's—was lack of rain. Objectively, neither RWU nor the ruling party could end the drought. Politically, however, they had to "do something" about it.

The use of watergates was made mandatory, necessitating the appointment of a Chief of Toilet Enforcement and hundreds of inspectors.

Criterion 2: Do It Now

When all hell is breaking loose, delay is tantamount to treachery. Waiting, pondering, or theorizing are subversion.*

If the luxury of pondering a solution is available, a crisis is *not* what a system faces.

Crisis Case X-2: The Trendy Heights Riot

A race riot erupted in the corridors and lunchroom of Trendy Heights High School.

The Trendy Heights school administrators acted swiftly. Any hesitation, they correctly feared, would be a signal to black militant leaders that the racial troubles were "going to be swept under the rug by the white power structure." Visions of picket signs and intemperate speeches filled the frightened heads of the school officials. They saw their careers stained by the label "racist." They had seen such troubles befall equivocating colleagues in other towns.

Something had to be done and done right away.

Two days after the riot the school board president announced that all Trendy Heights school district employees—teachers, officials, and janitors alike—would take part in a mandatory eight-hour Race Relations Professional Seminar.

Subsequently, racial attitude was incorporated as a criterion for hiring and promotion in the district. A new Human Resources Coordinator conducted a permanent series of Race Relations Workshops and directed the annual Black Culture Week.

Criterion 3: Do It Big

A subtle remedy is, in effect, no remedy at all. With no true solution at hand, do it big enough to be seen by all. In a crisis, the search is not for wisdom but for visibility.

Crisis Case X-3: The Great Swine Flu Epidemic

The slightest hint of spreading disease is fuel for outright

---

* Perversely, forming a task force to study a crisis is seen not as the delaying tactic it is but as morally acceptable "doing something."

panic. The report of four cases of swine flu on an Army base quickly became the Great Swine Flu Epidemic. Epidemics are crises of the first order. Any official who trifles with them is marked for a short career.

Few should have been surprised to find the Public Health Service responding to the first report of swine flu with a frenzy of righteous dictates. The Great Swine Flu Epidemic was tackled with a program of mass inoculations. Rarely have the unforeseen consequences of a rush to "do something" been so clear so soon. The supply of vaccine quickly ran out. Then came reports that some people had fallen ill from swine flu shots. A few died.

But what else could public-health officialdom have done? Suppose the first four swine flu cases had become a bona fide epidemic. Facing a choice between controversy and dishonor, only a fool would come down on the side of dishonor.

The Organizing Response

The "something" that impetuous administrators and officials do in a crisis is to organize. Not to organize in response to acute adversity is to forgo the immediate visibility of a committee, an emergency task force, or a coordinating office.

Crisis Case Z-1: Chock Full o' Promulgations

Emergency: A jet liner of Air Boravia was parked overnight at Regiment City International Airport. Because the ground crew, incredibly enough, forgot to chock the plane's wheels, a breeze started the plane rolling down the slight incline toward RC International's main runway. The good news was that its journey was interrupted when the front wheel struck an aircraft-handling tractor. The bad news was that the nose gear collapsed and the nose crashed to the pavement.

Morally Acceptable Response: A new Standard Operating

Procedure for parking aircraft at Regiment City International Airport was promulgated. Chocking wheels received special attention.

Crystallization: The new procedure requires the Assistant Airport Manager for Flight Services to inspect each parked aircraft personally and certify that each plane is safely chocked. The duty may not be delegated to a subordinate.

One lapse breeds permanent chores.

CRISIS CASE Z-2: MUTCHADOO ABOUT UTILITIES CONSERVATION

Emergency: The Arab oil boycott.

Morally Acceptable Response: Establish a faculty-staff-student committee on conserving electricity and fuel oil as clear evidence of Mutchadoo State University's contribution to making America "energy-independent."

Crystallization: The MSU Utilities Conservation Board quickly created the full-time post of Utilities Control Manager to enforce the board's policies. The first of these was University Instruction 11300.1A, a piece of Shiftscheme craftsmanship setting maximum temperatures for each MSU building and for each category of room use. Thereafter, the board distributed self-adhesive reminders to turn off lights and close windows.

CRISIS CASE Z-3: CATTLE POISONING IN MICHIGAN

Emergency: A fire retardant, known as PBB, found its way into a widely used animal feed in Michigan. Animals were poisoned; consumers shunned the state's agricultural products; farmers and meat-packers were in financial ruin.

Morally Acceptable Response: The state legislature created a ten-member Toxic Substance Control Board to monitor the use of toxic chemicals. The Detroit *Free Press* hailed the creation of the board as "an impressive first step" even before it had begun to operate.

Crystallization: The law establishing the board directed it to compile data on all toxic substances in the state, issue reports on toxic substances, coordinate national and state toxic control efforts, and alert state authorities to any toxic substance emergency.

Even casual readers will note that those legislated duties are beyond the capacity of ten commissioners. Experienced observers of organizations will agree that Michigan will soon have scores of inspectors, auditors, chemists, administrators, and publicists in the employ of the Toxic Substances Control Board.

One chance error breeds an army of functionaries, who, despite their numbers, cannot prevent a recurrence of the error.

CRISIS CASE Z-4: THAT DROUGHT IN BORAVIA AGAIN

Emergency: No rain for three years.

Morally Acceptable Response: Create an emergency Water Management Agency.

Crystallization: The temporary Water Management Agency expired eighteen months after the drought was ended by torrential rains that ravaged Boravian valleys with flooding. The temporary agency was then replaced by a permanent Ministry of Water Management Control.

Fix into Fixture

The final consequences of Emergency Shiftscheme Responses is to fatten, complicate, and rigidify.

No thoughtful student of unintended consequences can do

aught but wince upon looking back at the Shiftscheme monuments left in the wake of the crude oil crisis.

Since the Shiftscheme Response is known to breed work for others, emergency Shiftscheme reactions to distress will evolve into Blunderfret or Turnstile routines.*

Whether Turnstile or Blunderfret, the final bureaucratic crystallization will do little to prevent another crisis or prepare the system to handle one when it does occur. Only the desperate or the deceived will embrace an emergency Shiftscheme Response as a genuine remedy for anything.

To advise a troubled administrator *not* to act in a crisis is, however, pointless. It is tantamount to advising him to leave things to chance. He must act. The downstream consequences, fatter organizations and calcified work systems, are unavoidable, inevitable, irresistible. It is ever so.

---

* What is true of Shiftscheme Responses here is often equally true of Firecracker Responses.

Chapter 18

Coping

How to Survive in the System

It is not the business of the botanist to eradicate the weeds.
Enough for him if he can tell us just how fast they grow.
—C. Northcote Parkinson

Leaving nothing to chance, human action leads unswervingly to permanent, enduring systems of formal authority. All worthwhile things must be organized. They would not survive otherwise. What has been organized must then be expanded. In the name of achieving predictable outcomes, despised uncertainty must be driven out of all pursuits. Who would have it any other way? Who would choose the path of risk, anxiety, and surprise?

Once people have tasted the benefits of the slightest directed order, there is no keeping them from the organizing recipe box. Soon enough, hunger for certainty draws them under the mischievous influence of the Potato Chip Imperative. Having over-organized, they plunge into the irreversible futility of the Quicksand Corollary. The early joy of organizing is finally displaced by the symptoms of over-organization: End-Means, Priority Split, Spin-Off, and attempted insulation from the outside world.

There is no end to it.

Spitting Against the Wind

Despite having been told that over-organization is inevitable, many people, nonetheless, ask if the rising tide of

formalization can be stemmed. The answer is an unequivocal No!

Hierarchies could not prevail if mankind abhorred them. While everyone curses "bureaucracy," no one can resist "organizing."

Rugged individualists insist that the formalization which cannot be stemmed can surely be escaped. Yet we know that no one can flee an over-organized society without employing the principles of specialization and hierarchy. Thereby do rugged individualists become committee heads.

The foolhardy, few in number and futile in effect, choose to stay and fight. People who fancy themselves anti-bureaucracy radicals are seldom consistent. While they attack some hierarchies, they do not attack hierarchy itself as a way to get things done. Indeed, some radicals are themselves prolific organizers.

The Dilemma

Nothing can be done to turn back the spread of hierarchical authority. Few want to. Yet, while formal organizations push back uncertainty and foster efficiency, they also constrain and mold those within their jurisdictions. Therein lies the dilemma. We want what organizations do *for* us but we want to escape what they do *to* us.

What Can Be Done?

Even if retreat is futile and sabotage counterproductive, it is still possible to protect oneself from the harshest edges of large systems.

While the distortion of formal systems is revealed in a Quicksand Corollary or an Internal Spin-Off, these are not the flesh and blood of bureaucracy. Rather, it is the actions of specific individuals responding and adapting to Breakloop scoreboards that alternately exasperate and amuse.

In studying the behavior of functionaries in Breakloop situations, we have noted the few tactics that help minimize the worst aspects of authority hierarchies. It is possible for a few people—regrettably, not everyone—to survive and even prosper in the midst of over-organization. A sure grasp of the carrots and sticks that propel Shiftschemes, Firecrackers, Blunderfrets, and Turnstiles can be turned to personal advantage.

Coping with Shiftschemes

The Problem: As promulgators of programs and directives, Shiftschemes inflict their fellow man with more work, more instructions, and more forms.

Tactic: The Prima Donna Counter-Response. While few sensible people will threaten to walk away from their jobs because a Shiftscheme has burdened them with another five-page monthly report, every authority hierarchy has *some* people who will. Indeed, they will do it with a vengeance. They are *Prima Donnas.*

Prima Donnas are widely known for being arrogant, complaining, finicky, demanding, and late for meetings.

While many daydream about getting their own sweet way in a system, Prima Donnas do it regularly. Yet Prima Donnas are not only tolerated, they are indulged. Never punished for ignoring a system's trivia, Prima Donnas are applauded by the very people who must shoulder the burden of Shiftscheme demands that the Prima Donnas refuse. The bureaucratic world accommodates Prima Donnas, works around their preferences and eccentricities, and compensates for their rejection of rules that don't suit them.

The canons for successful Prima Donna Counter-Response are five in number. If even one is violated, the presentation is endangered.

1. Prima Donnas are born, not made. It would be suicide for an Obedient Fellow suddenly to assume the airs of a Prima Donna.

2. An organization can tolerate only a limited number of Prima Donnas. A hierarchy can be destroyed by ego overload in its authority circuits.

3. Prima Donnas must be competent. Genius helps; mediocrity will not suffice.

4. Prima Donnas must be predictable. Eccentricity will be tolerated only if it is not erratic. Obedient Fellows will get out of a Prima Donna's path, but only if they can calculate his trajectory.

5. Prima Donnas must keep a low profile. They can complain or demand; they cannot boast. Bragging encourages Obedient Fellows to try arrogance for themselves. Moreover, crowing about getting one's own way invites supervisory retaliation.

The Prima Donna Counter-Response is not for everyone. Many will immediately dismiss this tactic as distasteful or irresponsible. Such a reaction is a clear sign that the path of arrogance is not for them. They must resign themselves to accepting the incremental burdens of busy Shiftschemes.

The Shiftscheme centerpiece of Dean Planworth's effort to draw students and faculty together at Precarious College was a directive requiring professors to take part in commencement exercises, dressed in full academic regalia. The learned Professor Buchmacher, author of five best-selling biographies and holder of three teaching awards, told the dean, in inspired phrasing, to "stick it!" No one on the administrative staff of Precarious College mentioned commencement to Professor Buchmacher again. When the good professor retired, the college named its new library the Buchmacher Learning Resources Center.

When Behemoth Conglomerated distributed its fabled plan for mandatory car pooling, Ableman, manager of the

Shuttlecock Division in Prairie Heights, threw it in his wastebasket. Every Behemoth plant, division, and subsidiary across the land complied with the car-pooling edict except the highly profitable Prairie Heights facility. In explaining Ableman's unpunished arrogance, Tinkergood, corporate director of personnel, said, "It's O.K. We are working around him. Car pooling is a good program and it won't be hurt just because Ableman doesn't get behind it."

Indeed it won't. Shiftschemes invariably "work around" Prima Donnas. Shiftschemes, after all, are not concerned that any one person does not comply with a program. They have long known that actual effects are beside the point. Successful Shiftschemes focus only on the appearance that a program is working.*

Coping with Firecrackers

The Problem: Less intrusive than Shiftschemes, Firecrackers still pose a headache to busy organization people. Firecrackers devise, concoct, and impose their flashy task forces, committees, and attention-getting gimmicks wherever they can. They are mostly a problem to budget-conscious bosses.

Tactic: The Bottom Line Approach. The only people who can control Firecrackers are their superiors. It is precisely the failure of many managers to define jobs adequately that compels some subordinates to undertake freewheeling pyrotechnics in pursuit of attention.

An offending Firecracker must be brought in, sat down, looked in the eye, and asked firmly about the proverbial bottom line. How will his hoopla make things better? Who will be benefited? Can the benefit be measured? How much will it cost? What's it all about, Alfie?

Thumptub, chief public information officer for the Min-

---

* That sort of finicky concern with total compliance is the behavior of Blunderfrets.

istry of Education, used advertisements in newspapers and on television to promote a pamphlet, *Illiteracy and You,* free to all who wrote requesting it. At the close of the fiscal year, Dr. Doubting, deputy minister of education for programs, called in Thumptub to review the *Illiteracy and You* project. Thumptub waxed enthusiastic about illiteracy as the educational challenge of the 1980s, saying that it would reflect well on the ministry to be in the forefront of a crusade against illiteracy. Dr. Doubting agreed that it would indeed reflect well, but in the meantime the project had cost $500,000. Moreover, most of the 2,052 people who had written to the ministry requesting the pamphlet were upper middle class and college graduates. Replied Thumptub, "You can't really apply those outdated factory measures to an important program that deals in intangibles." Thumptub was posted as education attaché with the diplomatic mission to the South Pole.

Coping with Blunderfrets

The Problem: While Shiftschemes and Firecrackers bother us from time to time, it is the Blunderfrets, the keepers of red tape and wielders of official stamps, who drive us to distraction all the time.

Tactic: The "Where Is It Written?" Interrogative. If frustrated by a Blunderfret, appeal to the rules. Ask, "Where is it written?" This need not be an offensive demand. One can be courteous and still ask what rule the Blunderfret can cite for his decision, what directive guides his handling of your case.

Surprisingly, Blunderfrets often haven't read the regulation they cite to justify their actions.

In coping with Blunderfrets, your aim must be to see the actual wording of cited rules. There are few official rules written so clearly and definitively that they cannot be interpreted in your favor. Reasonable men can disagree about the intent or meaning of any directive.

No Blunderfret will unilaterally risk interpreting official directives. He has too much to lose. But if his supervisor examines a particular clause and agrees that your reading of it might be correct, the Blunderfret will readily go along. He is then off the hook; if things should go wrong later, it will be his boss's fault, not his.

Sezhoo approaches Balkside, clerk in the shoe department of Entrepot Emporium, to return a defective pair of shoes bought the day before.

BALKSIDE: I can't take them back. I don't recall that they were torn when you bought them. You probably laced them too tightly.

SEZHOO: Why can't you take them?

BALKSIDE: Store policy forbids it; you've already worn them. If you've worn them, I can't take them back.

Sezhoo thereupon takes the shoes to the assistant store manager, who refunds Sezhoo's money without hesitation in the name of another store policy, the one about serving the customer above all else. Balkside is relieved to have the decision taken out of his hands.

When Blunderfrets follow the rules with tedious precision they are maddening enough. How much more exasperating are they when they go *beyond* the rules to justify their procedures and responses according to rules that are of their making.

The first thing to be understood about Blunderfrets is that it is not in the nature of their jobs to promulgate procedures, write rules, or invent paperwork. Such creative work is exclusively the province of Shiftschemes. Higher management promulgates, Blunderfrets carry out.

In the event a Blunderfret cites a rule of his own making, your tactic must be different.

Making up the rules as he goes along puts a Blunderfret

in the untenable position of violating the bureaucratic principle of specialization. Such behavior is not characteristic of Blunderfrets, aversive to risk as they are, but it is common enough.

Coping with Turnstiles

The Problem: At first glance, busy Turnstiles seem not to be a problem at all. A low profile is in the nature of their work. They do not make sweeping promulgations like the Shiftschemes, undertake hoopla like the Firecrackers, or annoy those around them like the Blunderfrets. Yet none of the other Breakloop Behavior Types distorts work systems so thoroughly, however invisibly, as the Turnstiles.

Tactic: Counterintelligence. The Labor Theory of Value greatly favors Turnstiles. Most people admire hard workers no matter what they are doing. Only the bosses of Turnstiles can possibly have difficulty with them.

A supervisor of Turnstiles must ask the tough questions, not of the Turnstiles directly, but of himself. Turnstiles maximize what their bosses count. They count the wrong things because their superiors emphasize the quantifiable in a quest for defensible decisions. When a supervisor seeks Behavior A—and exhorts his subordinates to it—yet distributes rewards according to calculable Behavior B, it is inevitable that Turnstiles will pay lip service to A while laboring to maximize B.

Coping with Turnstiles begins at home.

While Sears, Roebuck & Company—like Demand Loop systems everywhere—encouraged its managers to contribute to maximum profits, the company unwittingly set up a Turnstile scoreboard called the 599 account. Sears established the 599 account in the 1950s as a small fund to absorb losses on unsold goods. Soon enough the size of the kitty became an end in itself, ballooning to $1 billion. The firm's buyers competed among themselves to contribute to the 599. According to the *Wall Street Journal,* the machinations of the account automatically raised Sears's purchasing costs and retail prices. The company progressively became less profitable and uncompetitive. Not until retail profits fell 23 percent in 1977 did Sears catch on to the mischief of Turnstile rewards for counting the wrong things.

Such antics must finally be arrested if a Demand Loop is to survive. In Breakloop systems Turnstiles maximize the wrong goals undiscovered, distorting organization behavior beyond the pale of intuitive diagnosis.

Understandably many readers will find such coping techniques distasteful or simply not applicable. Our advice is void where inhibited.

The If Only Moral

It is something of a tradition for sages of organization to conclude chapter upon chapter of clever insight with grand solemnity by tut-tutting the reader with the *If Only Moral.* The world such authors present doesn't exist, but it could *if only* mankind adhered to the prescriptions they expound.

If only the men and women who work in large organizations or deal with formal institutions would embrace the author's Vision X, renouncing their all-too-human Behavior Y, then, the Moral goes, the world would be a better place. Odious bureaucracy would shrivel before sunset *if only* reasonable minds accepted the Word as revealed by the author.

Haga's Law readily suggests numerous If Onlys.

If only people would stop maximizing the wrong things in the popular Turnstile mode, workmanship would improve and organizations would assume a humane climate of which only a few have dared to dream.

If only the souls who toil in Blunderfret jobs would lose themselves in a riot of free spiritedness, hierarchies everywhere would become helpful beyond description.

If only decision makers would work up a frenzy of awareness, they could foresee, and thereby avoid, the absurdities of Shiftscheme Responses.

If only planners would carefully think through the long-run consequences of Priority Splits and Spin-Offs, the costs of bloated administration would be halved.

If only *you* could transcend Breakloop dynamics, resist Potato Chip Imperatives, keep from tumbling into Quicksand Corollaries, and exorcise the Labor Theory of Value, then benefactions would surely be visited upon mankind. Without doubt they surely would.

If only.

The Central Point

Fortified with the knowledge that few people, indeed, are about to overturn the realities and constraints of organized systems, we have resisted sermonettes on the If Only Moral.

People won't because they can't.

If they did, they would be leaving things to chance.

The central point of Haga's Law is that humanity prefers to leave nothing to chance.

"De-Organize the World!" is a seductive battle cry, drawing many into a futile fray against the demon hierarchy. Yet, while a few shallow Quixotes are pasting "De-Organize" stickers on their car bumpers, the itch to organize is spreading. Indeed, some organizing will be needed to produce the bumper stickers, to assure their wide distribution, and to arrange for "De-Organize the World!" speakers' appearances on TV talk shows.

Inevitably, some enthusiast will found a National Association for the De-Organization of the World, which will finally succumb to the temptations of Haga's Law.

Attempting to turn back the rising tide of organizing would mean letting things be. It would mean taking risks. It would mean leaving things to chance, which would create anxiety. And anxiety, of course, breeds organizing. The organizing will breed new anxieties, which will be met by further organizing. There is no end to it.

Acknowledgments

After completing the first drafts of the manuscript we have been repeatedly dismayed to come upon lucid and powerful statements of ideas we had labored to explain and illustrate. In every case, however, our current consternation has been overshadowed by our original distress at how little the prior writings on over-organization and its consequences seem to inform crucial decisions made every day, whether in Cabinet rooms or living rooms. At every level, otherwise sophisticated people are unwittingly caught up in such obvious traps as the Potato Chip Imperative. Intelligent and reasonable people concoct such organizational cow pies as Turnstile Adaptation scoreboards with no concept of the easily predictable dysfunctions that invariably follow.

In all likelihood this book does not contain a single original idea. Even the ideas that we fancy are our very own will probably turn out to be conceits fostered by poor memories or careless notes. Many have said what we say—and many among them have said it better. It is their light that we want to get out from under their academic bushel.

A heavy debt is owed to those whose ideas we have borrowed, repackaged, and put out to market. Joseph Litterer has forcefully sketched the unrelenting trend of all human relations toward formalization.[1] James March and Herbert Simon, of course, are the explicit source of what we call the Priority Split.[2] Having worked out the idea of the Spin-Off Effect in its many variations on our own, we then discovered that Victor Thompson, in a slim but powerful volume, had anticipated us in that as well as in the Shiftscheme Response.[3] Jay Forrester is the source of our concern about the hazards of applying commonsense remedies to the problems of large, complex systems that are invisibly counterintuitive.[4] Robert LeFevre's writings contributed to our concept of Breakloop systems.[5] Ludwig von Mises also developed the idea of Breakloop systems in his distinction between payers and users in nonmarket systems.[6] Robert Merton is well known for his work on the unforeseen consequences of inverting ends and means in bureaucracies.[7] The distorting effect of specific quantitative work goals—what we call the Turnstile Adaptation—has been previously revealed in Peter Blau's celebrated study of government employment offices.[8] Many of the insights scattered throughout *Haga's Law* are here because the same insights are also scattered throughout the collaborative work of Daniel Katz and Robert Kahn.[9] The very notion that organization problems are not just people problems writ large (but are problems of the shape and workflow of organizations themselves) has been received from the iconoclastic influence of Charles Perrow.[10]

Many people have encouraged and assisted the writing of *Haga's Law* and it would not exist without them. The first impetus to write the book at all came from students in the Analysis of Bureaucracy course at the Naval Postgraduate School in Monterey. Leon Hayden was particularly insistent that these ideas must reach a larger audience. What we have finally produced may not be at all what he or they had in mind.

Once the book was begun, curiosity and gentle prodding from friends and colleagues coaxed it toward completion. The urgings and interest of Robert Whiteside, David C. Burns, Michael K. Block, Ralph Hummel, Pat Boughton, Alfred Schenkman, and Ted Taylor were crucial at various junctures.

A hearty thanks is owed to Sunny Matteson, Sharon Foust,

and Cathy Ochsenrider for helping to prepare early drafts of the chapters. Jean Casko expeditiously typed the entire final manuscript so that we met our deadlines.

Words in print cannot express what we owe to the two unsparing critics but patient souls to whom this book is dedicated, Carline Kirtz Haga and Joan Ross Acocella.

[1] Joseph A. Litterer, *Organizations: Structure and Behavior,* Volume I, second edition. New York: John Wiley and Sons, 1969.

[2] James G. March and Herbert A. Simon with the collaboration of Harold Guetzkow, *Organizations.* New York: John Wiley and Sons, 1958.

[3] Victor A. Thompson, *Without Sympathy or Enthusiasm: The Problem of Administrative Compassion.* University, Ala.: University of Alabama Press, 1975.

[4] Jay W. Forrester, "Counterintuitive Behavior of Social Systems," *Reason,* Vol. 3, Nos. 4 and 5, July and August, 1971; reprinted from January, 1971, issue of *Technology Review,* published by the Alumni Association of the Massachusetts Institute of Technology.

[5] Robert LeFevre, "The Structure: A Derivative of the Longing for Immortality," *Rampart Journal,* Vol. 3, No. 4, Winter, 1967; "The Anatomy of Structure," *Rampart Journal,* Vol. 4, No. 2, Summer, 1968.

[6] Ludwig von Mises, *Bureaucracy.* New Haven: Yale University Press, 1944.

[7] Robert K. Merton, *Social Theory and Social Structure,* revised. New York: The Free Press, 1957.

[8] Peter M. Blau, *The Dynamics of Bureaucracy,* revised edition. Chicago: University of Chicago Press, 1963.

[9] Daniel Katz and Robert L. Kahn, *The Social Psychology of Organizations.* New York: John Wiley and Sons, 1966.

[10] Charles Perrow, *Organizational Analysis: A Sociological View.* Monterey: Brooks/Cole, 1970.